MW01286749

The Art of Good Enough

All Things Women

CREATE THE LIFE YOU LOVE

THE WORKING MOM'S
GUILT-FREE GUIDE TO THRIVING
WHILE BEING *perfectly imperfect*

The ART of Good enough.

DR. IVY GE

Copyright © 2020 Ivy Ge

All rights reserved. No part of this publication may be reproduced, distributed, or transmitted in any form or by any means, including photocopying, recording, or other electronic or mechanical methods, without the prior written permission of the publisher, except in the case of brief quotations embodied in critical reviews and certain other noncommercial uses permitted by copyright law.

The Art of Good Enough is a work of nonfiction. Nonetheless, some of the names and personal characteristics of the individuals involved have been changed in order to disguise their identities. Any resulting resemblance to persons living or dead is entirely coincidental and unintentional.

ISBN: 978-1-64085-952-4 (hardcover)
ISBN: 978-1-64085-951-7 (paperback)
ISBN: 978-1-64085-953-1 (ebook)

Library of Congress Control Number: 2019914424

Excerpt from UCSF Magazine (page 114, 115, 116)
Reprinted by permission

Editing by Candace Johnson, Change It Up Editing
Front cover image by HikkO/99 Designs
Interior design by JetLaunch
Author photo by Elisa Cicinelli

First printing edition 2020

To request a bulk order discount, email Contact@ivyge.com

Printed in the United States of America
Published by Author Academy Elite
PO Box 43, Powell, OH 43035
www.AuthorAcademyElite.com

Visit https://ivyge.com/the-art-of-good-enough/

To women who are still figuring it out

Contents

The Path

Introduction

Have you ever lain awake wondering if you're a bad mother? If you've done everything you could to keep your children happy, healthy, and to maximize their chances of success? From your in-laws to the women in the park, everyone has a firm grip on what a good mother does, except you. As you listen to your partner snoring away blissfully in the dark, you wonder why you feel like a failure even though you've done a million things from dawn to dusk with never a moment of peace. How can your partner sleep like a baby every night, not bothered by the mile-long to-do list for tomorrow? How can he tell you to relax and everything will be okay, when you're overwhelmed, underappreciated, and terribly lonely?

You're not alone.

Working mother is the most demanding role in modern society. It demands endless patience, infinite adaptability, and the incredible balancing act of a high-wire walker between the towers of career and motherhood.

Every single day.

Before becoming mothers, we were girls with dreams. We had silly jokes. We watched the sunset and listened to the wind. We were wholesome then. With motherhood, our lives are divided into slices, filled with appointments, activities, homework, housework, and family obligations. There's little time left for our dreams and silly jokes. We stop our gym memberships, skip the girls' nights out, put aside our hobbies; we settle on the easiest hairstyles; we eat whatever is available in the fridge; we are determined to be the best moms we can. We carry the burden of responsibilities, heads down, putting one foot in front of the other on the long journey toward the temple of perfection. Despite all the good intentions, time, and effort we devote to this noble position, we aren't sure if we have done enough or whether our kids will turn out all right.

Technology has made life much easier than decades ago, yet more moms feel anxious and inadequate than ever. The more connections we have online, the fewer people we can talk to about our overwhelming sense of failure. Behind the happy family posts we share with the world, there are moments we wonder how much longer we can do this, day after day, year after year.

We become invisible in the frantic race to meet everyone's needs. We don't like what we see in the mirror—the relentless wrinkles and sagging skin. We don't like what we feel about our bodies—easily tired, out of shape, and worst of all, we find little joy in caring for our partners and children. Yes, we love them, but is love enough to keep us marching on this motherhood pilgrimage?

One chilly afternoon in early 2005, I sat in a small exam room at the University of California San Francisco (UCSF) Student Health Clinic and told the nurse practitioner I couldn't handle it anymore. I was a second-year student in the best pharmacy school in the country. My son, Ethan, was almost six months old. He had asthma that required a nightly nebulizer treatment. For the machine to work properly, I had to hold him in my arms at night to keep him at a reclining angle rather than lying flat in his crib. I did my homework at 3:00 a.m. and then went to school at 7:00 a.m. on weekdays. I worked on the weekends for money to buy cute outfits for Ethan.

My husband, Chu, and I had bought a house the year before. He worked full time, paying for the mortgage, my tuition, and our living expenses. I had packed on twenty pounds from the pregnancy and couldn't fit into any of my old clothes, so I continued wearing the baggy pregnancy garb, not wanting to spend any more money on myself. I felt awful most of the time: I was sleep deprived, unable to concentrate, and worried about Ethan, my grades, and the endless house-work at home. Chu helped me with the baby as much as he could. We bickered frequently, arguing about whose turn it was to do the chores.

The nurse practitioner listened to my problems patiently. He was a man in his fifties with gray hair and wise eyes. He advised me with all seriousness that I should replace my broken dishwasher with a new one. "Come back to see me again if you still have problems after getting a new dishwasher," he said.

I was falling apart, and a dishwasher wasn't going to fix me.

After the visit, I spent days considering my options: I could quit pharmacy school or consider postponing it until Ethan was older. Becoming a pharmacist was the career change I had been waiting for, after working for an airline with degrees in business and engineering. I could stop working and use precious weekend hours to catch up on studying. I could also give up on being a good mother. I was ill-prepared for motherhood; I didn't know what to do most of the time, so I constantly worried if I would ruin Ethan's life. All of my options involved giving up something to regain control of my life. Which one of them would be my best bet? I didn't want to be just a mother; I wanted an identity beyond motherhood. For all the ingenious women before me, there must be something out there that could guide me through the mess. I wanted to look good and feel good while having a happy family and a successful career.

Fast forward to 2015: I became one of the first 500 clinical pharmacists in the country with dual board certifications in pharmacotherapy and critical care. In 2018, Ethan was accepted into the best public high school in San Francisco. Chu and I are still married and living in the same house. We never replaced the broken dishwasher.

I discovered the key to being a happy, healthy, and confident working mother is to make choices based on my values and only strive for what is good enough for me.

Since 2005, I have continued my search for mind and body transformation methods that work for working moms who have little time and resources. I read hundreds of books, studied cutting edge research findings in neurobehavioral, psychological, and social science. I experimented with different techniques of self-improvement and developed easy and effective practices that keep me focused and efficient. I tried out various workout routines, and I worked with personal trainers and sports professionals to find the one best suited for my body type and lifestyle. My beauty and fitness routines help me maintain a youthful look and an hourglass figure. Just last week, a guy in his twenties asked me out during my lunch-hour walk. When I told him I'm happily married and my son is in high school, he didn't believe me.

I condensed everything I've learned into these pages. There are three sections in the book. The Mind focuses on discovering your strengths and transforming the way you think and act. The Body illustrates understanding and working with your body to improve your health and confidence. The Path centers on pursuing a meaningful life beyond motherhood. Throughout the book, I mention the importance of self-monitoring, from relieving emotional strains to understanding how your body changes to appreciating your growth in reaching the goals. This book's companion journal is a multifunctional tool designed for you to complete these steps to the life you love. If you want to learn more about the strategies discussed in this book, visit my website https://ivyge.com for the related free online course offering.

Every technique I show you is proven feasible and effective with little time and resources required. That doesn't mean you'll flip through these pages and become a new person at the end of the book. Knowing something but not doing anything with it is a waste of that knowledge. Practicing the techniques I show you for a few minutes a day is all it takes. The more time you devote to the practice, the faster you'll see the results.

There are many ways to achieve a worthy goal in life. The most satisfying and long-lasting approach is to give a little effort every day. As with any great success in life, time is the most enduring witness of our journey to fulfillment.

Everything you need for your mind and body transformation is already in you. My job is to show you how to find it, enhance it, and use it to create your best life.

THE MIND

Your mind is your compass;
What you see dictates how you feel;
What you focus on determines what you'll achieve;
Look within you for strengths; look around you for beauty.

1

What's Good Enough?

PERFECTION IS LIKE infinity; it's a great concept but impossible to reach. We can't strive for perfection without feeling defeated, questioning our intelligence and ability. If you want a happy, healthy, and confident self, stop chasing the unobtainable. Take an inventory of your life, and examine the pattern perpetuating your disappointment. Ask yourself, *Can I break the negative cycle for a better outcome?* If you see no way out of your current situation, you haven't looked closely enough. You hold the key to your own problems. I'll show you how to uncover your strengths and hidden wealth to map out the path to the life you deserve.

The Distance Between Pleasure and Pain

There are only two types of goals in life: moving toward pleasure or moving away from pain. Those who move toward pleasure know what they want and make efforts to reach their rewards. When they encounter pain on their journey, they see it as necessary before their favorable outcomes. Those who move away from pain live their lives passively, letting fear guide their courses of action. Although they minimize the risk of failure, they're far from success.

Which one of these are you?

Your goal determines your path. You don't change your goal; the past only reinforces the future. If you want a new life, set a new goal. Stop playing all the worst-case scenarios in your head. You don't need the entire map drawn out before taking the first step. When you drive at night, you can only see as far as your headlights allow. As the road extends before you, you find your way to the destination.

The key to your desired outcome is to have the right goal. This goal must be long-term, obtainable, and aligned with your values. Short-term goals are specific to the stage of your life. They don't provide further guidance once you achieve them. Obtainability means you don't aim for perfection; you aspire to reach your full potential. Alignment with your values means you live in tune with who you are. Living by other people's values won't make you happy, even when those values belong to your loved ones.

Most people know what they don't want. Few can tell you what they do want. Before you set a worthy goal, ask yourself what is important in your life. Recall the events in your life; what made you proud despite failures? What left you wanting more even when you succeeded? Your goal should not be defined by the life you lived but by the unlived life within you. Think about the dreams you ignored because of the circumstances, the marriage, the kids, and the job. Pay attention to what you yearn for ... who you want to be.

The art of good enough has two layers of meaning. One, define the standard you consider good based on your values. It should be consistent in all aspects of your life. Inconsistency in action will confuse you and lead you astray from the path to your desired outcome. Two, our time and energy are limited. We have to be misers to the things that don't matter to us and give abundance to what does matter. Every time you struggle to decide, ask yourself if it will matter to you in five years, in ten years. If the answer is no, don't give it another thought. Life is too short to dwell on background noises. We only fight the battles worthy of our time and effort.

Maximize Your Happiness

Take a look at the area where the three circles overlap; that is where happiness resides. Health represents the emotional and physical well-being; connection means maintaining harmonious personal and social relationships; satisfaction indicates internal gratification.

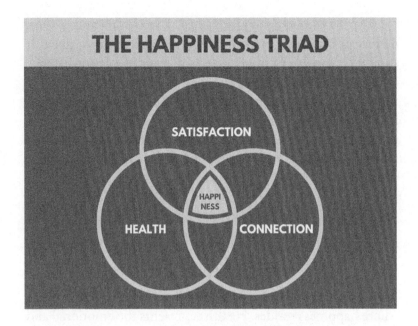

We feel happy when we achieve emotional and physical well-being, meaningful connections, and satisfaction. All three components have to be in balance with each other to maximize happiness.

When we devote all our waking hours to caring for our children and partners, the circle of connection expands while the areas of satisfaction and health shrink. As a result, the area of happiness becomes much smaller. We feel stressed out, angry, and lonely. In return, the quality of our care declines. Our maximal efforts yield suboptimal performance.

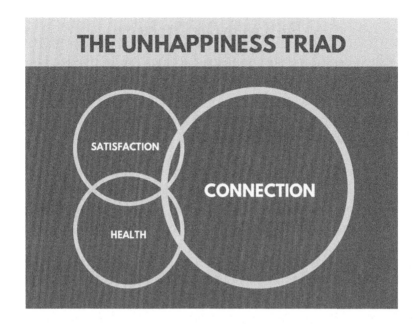

Contrary to common beliefs, putting your children and partner first at all times isn't the best way to love them. Scheduling routine "me time" to regain a sense of control is not being selfish. It's essential for our well-being.

It's impossible to take good care of others when you don't care about yourself. You might pull it off for a short while, but in the long run, the burden on your mind turns into pains and ailments in your body. You take medications to ease the physical symptoms, which gives you new sets of problems from the adverse effects of the pills. Being a hospital pharmacist for over a decade, I've seen many cases like this. Take care of yourself before it's too late, for the sake of your family and friends. Remember, you and your partner are the role models for your children. If you don't maintain a healthy lifestyle, how do you expect your kids to pick up the good habits?

The Key to Our Problems

When describing our problems to others, we emphasize how difficult our children are, how unappreciative our partners get, and how demanding our jobs become. Rather than waiting for others to change, think about how you can influence them in a positive direction.

Children didn't decide to be difficult one day. Our parenting approach may have played a role in their behaviors. Kids learn fast, especially from the people they spend the most time with. Since this is a whole topic on its own, I'll address child-rearing issues in Chapter 10.

You wanted to have children with your partner for a good reason. What has changed in the relationship since the births of your little pumpkins? How often do you talk to each other about your feelings? When was the last time you had sex that made you feel like a woman in love? Chapter 9 will tell you how to nurture the most important relationship in your life.

Once you figure out how to care for your kids and partner wisely, you'll feel more energetic at work, more poised to handle challenging tasks. Your positive attitude will attract more opportunities.

The Path to Happiness, Health, and Confidence

There are four steps to draw up your own success blueprint:

Step One: Define Where You Are and Where You Want to Be

1. Discover your values and strengths (Chapters 2 and 3)
2. Revisit your old dreams (Chapter 18)
3. Prepare for your transformation (Chapters 4 and 8)
4. Look good and feel better (Chapters 11, 12, 13, 14)

Step Two: Declutter Your Life

1. Live simply (Chapter 4)
2. Declutter your mind (Chapters 6 and 7)
3. Recharge your body (Chapters 16 and 17)

Step Three: Build a Support Network

1. Bring passion to your relationship (Chapters 9 and 15)
2. Raise independent children (Chapter 10)
3. Rally for support (Chapter 21)

Step Four: Create the Life You Love

1. Reverse engineer your path (Chapter 19)
2. Maximize your productivity (Chapter 20)
3. Be prepared for the journey to success (Chapter 22)

To present the above information in an easy to follow manner, I grouped them in three sections titled "The Mind," "The Body," and "The Path," respectively. In the next few chapters I will illustrate Steps One through Three in detail, together with various methods to help you overcome the negative emotions keeping you from living your best life. After you have a firm grip on what you need to create the life you love and how to focus your energy on important things, I'll show you how to get healthy and look and feel your best in "The Body." Once your confidence improves, we'll revisit all the steps in "The Path" to reverse engineer your path to the life you deserve.

2

How Well Do You Know Yourself?

LIFE IS A sequence of choices we make. What we hold on to and what we let go of make all the difference.

Before we know what we want, we must know who we are. Yet knowing ourselves is among the hardest things to do these days. Our lives are packed with responsibilities and distractions, leaving little room to reflect on what is meaningful to us. We're busy reacting rather than living, looking at but not seeing the truth in life. Until one day when our health breaks down and we finally stop to ponder what is important to us and how we should live the rest of our lives.

Some of you may say you know yourself well. You've done the Myers-Briggs personality test or the 16 Personalities questionnaire.[1] Yes, these analyses provide insights into our temperament and behavioral characteristics. But we change in reaction to the changes in our environment. If you did your test back in those college years, I'm not sure how accurate it'll be now. Think of these tests as photos taken at a particular moment of your life—a glimpse of your past.

Most people know their weaknesses well; few know their strengths. Ever since we were old enough to tell right from wrong, we learned about our shortcomings, often from our parents. They wanted to protect us by informing us about what we lacked and the importance of amelioration. We were told to work on our weaknesses so we could increase our chances of success.

The thing is, if we only focus on our weaknesses, that is all we see, so we feel insecure, and believe we're not good enough. All you working mothers out there, if you remember one thing from this book, let it be this message: it's much more satisfying and effective to enhance our strengths than to improve our weaknesses.

Nicole Kidman, a renowned actor and producer, describes herself as being exceptionally shy, a circumstance that was only worsened by her childhood stutter. "I just remember everyone always saying to me, 'Calm down, think about what you're gonna say.'" Even with her massive success in the entertainment business, "I don't like walking into a crowded restaurant by myself."[2] Our genetic makeup has created a blueprint for us, where our weaknesses and strengths are laid out already. Our job is to figure out how to maximize the effect of our strengths while not letting our weaknesses stop us. No one is perfect, so we can shove off the burden of trying to be so.

What Are My Strengths?

Few of us know precisely in what areas we excel because we've been focusing on improving our weaknesses. Strengths lead us to new horizons; our flaws keep us on the treadmill of life, busy running but not getting anywhere. To have an accurate grasp of your strengths requires work, but the result will be empowering. When you know the *magic* words that sum up the purpose of your life, you'll know why you've failed in previous attempts trying to fit. Instead of muscling with your feebleness, you can now free yourself of that burden and discover where your strengths can lead you.

The four steps of self-discovery include:

1. Think deeply about yourself.
2. Reflect on your past interests that weren't fueled by monetary benefits.
3. Think about what others say about you.
4. Use a well-tested character strengths assessment tool to verify your findings.

Think Deeply about Yourself

What activities energize you? What gives you joy just thinking about it? When are you at your best? Periodically take an inventory of your emotions, filter out the impurities, and look for the gold specs that highlight your life.

My husband had trouble deciding what career he should pursue when he finished high school. All his friends wanted the computer science major as it was all the rage in the '90s. He took a week-long road trip to Yellowstone National Park. The open road and scenery helped him think deeply about what he cared about the most and what he was good at. When he returned, he chose to study civil engineering. While many of his friends switched career during the dot-com crash in the early 2000s, he's still satisfied with his career path.

Reflect on Your Past Interests that Weren't Fueled by Monetary Benefits

Think about what you wanted to be when you were in tenth grade. What activities consumed most of your time when you were a child? I've loved reading from a very young age. By the time I was twelve, I had read all the classic literature on my father's bookshelves, such as *War and Peace*, *Crime and Punishment*, and Walt Whitman's *Leaves of Grass*. I was enthralled by the power of words. I had a big pile of notebooks collecting all the beautiful phrases I encountered. I wrote my first novel when I was ten. My parents told me I needed to have a successful career to be financially stable. So I tried a business major, then engineering, and eventually pharmacy. Although I've published technical articles and research papers, creative writing was always a nostalgic thought for me.

A few years ago, a surgery kept me off work for weeks. During those long, idle days, I started writing a political thriller. I watched my characters react and then fight back as their lives turned upside down. I cried for their struggles and their courage to do the right thing. I haven't stopped writing since.

Think about What Others Say about You

We're not always the best judges of our characters. Others may have a more accurate view of our personality traits. Your close friends and family members will be among the first people you'll want to consult. I asked my seven-year-old son what he thought of me. Amazingly, he identified three of my top five strengths. If you have trusted colleagues at work, ask them what you have done well. These external inputs will converge on a few core characteristics that likely represent your inner wealth.

You may receive a range of opinions about you from different sources, so the caveat is to find commonality in them. Reflect on your past experience to verify the existence of such traits. Ignore those irrelevant statements about you. You don't live according to people's opinions. You live true to your values.

Use a Well-Tested Character Strengths Assessment Tool to Verify Your Findings

Drs. Christopher Peterson and Martin Seligman, two well-known researchers in positive psychology, created the Values in Action Signature Strengths test to help people identify their own positive strengths and learn how to capitalize on them. The questionnaire contains 240 questions that take about twenty-five minutes to complete. You can register and take the full test at www.authentichappiness.org for free and receive feedback on your top five strengths.

The survey examines an individual's profile of character strengths in the following categories:

Wisdom and Knowledge: creativity, curiosity, judgment, love of learning, perspective

Courage: bravery, perseverance, honesty, zest

Humanity: love, kindness, emotional intelligence

Justice: teamwork, fairness, leadership

Temperance: forgiveness, humility, prudence, self-regulation

Transcendence: appreciation of beauty and excellence, gratitude, hope, humor, spirituality

My top three strengths are *love of learning, fairness, and curiosity.*

Once you have identified your strengths, view them as the clues to your struggles and untapped potentials. In the next chapter, I'll show you how to improve the fit between your strengths and your life.

Top Strengths

(1) Spirituality, sense of purpose, and faith

(2) self-control and self-regulation

(3) judgment, critical thinking, and open-mindedness

(4) industry, diligence, and perseverance

(5) caution, prudence, and discretion

Top Weaknesses

(1) (weakest) citizenship, teamwork, & loyalty

(2) modesty and humility

(3) forgiveness and mercy

(4) humor and playfulness

(5) kindness and generosity

My top virtue categories:
① transcendence (spirituality)
② temperance (self-regulation)
③ wisdom (judgment)
④ courage (perseverance)
⑤ temperance (prudence)

3

Improve the Fit Between Your Strengths and Your Life

EVERY ONE OF us lives three lives simultaneously: public life, personal life, and private life. Your sense of happiness depends on the level of harmony among these lives.

↑ In other words:
① faith
② self-regulation (self-control)
③ wisdom (I make decisions based on objective truth.)
④ courage (I persist toward my goals despite discouragements.)
⑤ prudence (I act carefully and cautiously, looking to avoid 23 unnecessary risks and planning with the future in mind.)

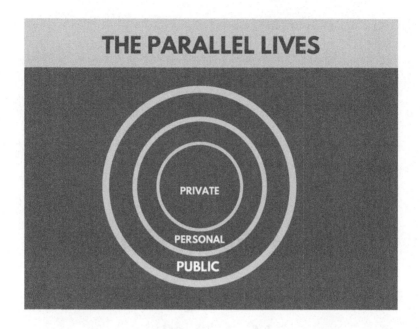

Your private life is your thoughts and beliefs. It's the smallest unit of all three lives, yet it determines the level of satisfaction you feel toward your other two lives. Your personal life is your circle of family and close friends. They are the pillars of your universe. When your private life fails to align with your personal life, you may experience resentment, anger, and likely physical pain. Your public life is where you interact with people outside of your personal life. It could be your job, social groups, religious organizations, and of course, social media. Most of us try to be our best in the public eye, highlighting what we have and covering up what we lack in our personal and private lives. When the gap between our public image and the truth enlarges, our happiness declines. We feel awful for two reasons: the pressure to keep up with what people expect of us, and the inability to change our personal and private lives.

With the social media boom comes the great irony: we keep posting our polished happy photos and stories when, in fact, we can barely hold on. The images we project and the number of likes and shares we get become the indicator of our worth. We are tormented by our desire to look good and feel proud. It's a chain we put around our own necks. We no longer live free and true to ourselves.

We have to break that chain.

All positive changes must originate from your private life and then propagate your personal life, and eventually your public life.

If you have been unhappy for a while, you get stuck in a thought pattern that every trivial thing happening to you confirms your suffering. The self-fulfilling prophecy of failure makes it more taxing to complete your tasks at work and at home. If you want to be happy, healthy, and confident, stop this negative belief. Think about how your strengths can help you overcome challenges more effectively.

I'll use my friend Helen as an example. To protect her and her family's privacy, I changed their names and other specifics.

Helen is a mother of eight-year-old twin girls. She works full time as a marketing associate at an advertising firm. Her husband, Jim, a construction contractor who works long hours, rarely offers help. Most of the weekdays, Helen does house chores late into the night, exhausted and lonely. Because of her busy schedule, she doesn't have time to play with her daughters, to cuddle, laugh, and be silly. After putting on fifteen pounds since the twins were born, Helen only buys shapeless clothes and has stopped putting on makeup altogether. She no longer goes out with her unmarried, fashionable friends. One day, she runs into an old college friend who doesn't recognize her because of her drastic change. She wants to talk to Jim about her struggle, but he falls asleep while she's still talking. She wonders what happened to the passionate Jim she married. She thought they were soulmates.

Helen loves her job, where she can express her creative talent. She dreams of running national campaigns for her firm's top clients. She's disciplined, organized, and efficient at work. Recently her boss offered her a manager position in charge of two of their biggest clients. She likes the challenge of handling large accounts but worries the longer work hours will make her a bad mom. Jim tells her to turn down the offer because he just signed a new contract, and coming home early is out of the question. Helen resents her lone sacrifice for the family. She yells at Jim and cries to sleep.

The next morning, Helen wakes up with a stiff neck. She feels depressed and lacks energy. When she helps her daughters with their homework in the evening, she yells at them because they don't get it after repeated explanations. The girls burst into tears. Helen hates herself.

She tells her boss she can't take the promotion because of her domestic responsibilities. Her boss gives her two weeks to think it over because the promotion means she will be the first female manager ever at the firm.

Working moms pursuing a career goal often feel guilty for choosing their careers over their children. Lack of support from their partners often makes them feel selfish going after something that only benefits themselves. In Helen's case, her confidence and job satisfaction is an essential part of her private life. Her personal life demands her time as a caregiver, which means long hours of cleaning and preparing with little intellectual stimulation. When these two lives pull her in different directions, she believes herself a failure, and her health deteriorates. The conflict between these two lives leads her to decline the promotion, a downturn in her public life.

How should Helen resolve the conflict between her private life and personal life, and subsequently achieve her career goal? Let's examine Helen's strengths: creativity, self-regulation, and caring. She's at the center of this tug-of-war: on one side lies her needs for a fulfilling career that highlights her creative talent; on the other side rests her need to love and be loved at home. How can she satisfy both needs without being torn in the middle?

After spending a week weighing her options, Helen goes back to her boss with a counteroffer. She'll take the promotion but wants to work only three days in the office while working from home for the rest of the week. Because of her organizational skills, she can collaborate with her colleagues on large projects efficiently while at home. Her boss hesitates, so she asks for a three-month tryout. If she doesn't deliver what she promised, she'll step down from her role. The boss accepts her proposal.

Helen talks with Jim about the possibility of hiring a part-time assistant to help him with time-consuming tasks so he can work less. Her increase in salary and bonuses with the manager position will more than offset the cost of such help. On her working days, Jim agrees to come home early and take care of the twins, but says he won't do housework.

Helen learns to ignore the urge to clean up the moment she steps into the house. She hires a cleaning service to come in once a week to keep the house in order. Helen proves herself at work and secures her promotion in three months. To celebrate, she buys a pair of major league baseball play-off tickets for Jim's birthday, and they have a great time at the game. When Jim thanks her for the surprise gift, Helen asks if he still loves her because she no longer feels his love. Her statement shocks Jim. He thought she'd been doing fine. Helen expresses her need to communicate with Jim just like before they had the twins. He promises to listen to her more and doesn't object when she wants to work out. Although there are still many issues to resolve, Helen is happy that Jim wants to make their relationship work.

Now it's your turn to examine the conflicts between your private, personal, and public lives. Figure out how to change these three lives based on your strengths. If you're stuck, check out the free online courses on my website for specific recommendations.

4

Stop Taking Yourself So Seriously

BEFORE YOU ATTEMPT any change to your life, the number one rule is to stop taking yourself so seriously.

Why? The more you want to protect and defend your old identity, the less likely you'll transform the way you think and act.

Women hang on to the bad things longer, question ourselves more often, and hold ourselves to incredibly higher standards than men could ever understand. Soon after the birth of a new baby and while still feeling the euphoria of new motherhood, we go back to work, taking on the hybrid position that requires 24/7 diligence despite mounting anxiety and the mind-numbing routine of bottles, diapers, and lack of sleep. When older children are involved, there's also homework, afterschool activities, and school projects to contend with.

Picture an overweight guy in his forties riding a shiny Harley motorcycle on the freeway with loud vroom and even louder pride. His arms are outstretched, his face beaming. Did he care that anyone is watching his love handle jutting out of his black muscle tank? Not at all. His mind is with the sun, the wind, and the open road in front of him. Now imagine yourself sitting on a Harley, giddy for the rare occasion of a joy ride. You like the feel of wind on your face, your hair dancing wildly. You feel young and free. Suddenly, you become aware of the breeze brushing against your midsection, and your mind zooms in on that jiggering sensation. Is your T-shirt lifted by the wind? How much of the muffin top can others see? You struggle to remain calm while looking for the next exit. No more freedom on this ride, you see?

The truth is, no one is watching you, at least not for long. Most of us are not that interesting. Social media makes us more fascinating than we deserve. The bar is set so high that it's stressful to measure up. Everyone else believes you're happy when you're in fact anxious and depleted. Think of the eclectic chef Anthony Bourdain, the talented fashion designer Kate Spade. Money and fame didn't help these celebrities live happily to their golden age, so why do you think those things would make you feel good?

You want a happier self? Stop taking yourself so seriously. Crack a joke about yourself if you can. No one is perfect, so why pretend? Superiority repels. The true masters make us ordinary people feel stronger and better than we are. Be genuine; it's easier to live that way. Research shows people find honesty and humor disarmingly likable. The thing with lies is that after you lie once, you'll have to keep lying to get the record straight until you hate yourself. Every lie and excuse you give is a brick you lay around yourself; eventually, the brick walls will box you in. Remember back in 2013, how Lance Armstrong finally admitted using banned performance-enhancing drugs in seven successive Tours de France after years of denying it?

Stop thinking about how others feel about you. Focus on how you feel, and figure out how you can feel better. Stop pleasing the people who only want you to look and behave in a certain way. They are not your true friends. If something makes you feel good, do it more often; if some people make you laugh, spend more time with them.

Don't be afraid to try new things. New experiences give you new perspectives, either about yourself or about life, and often both. Psychologist Rich Walker of Winston-Salem State University studied 30,000 event memories and over 500 diaries, and concludes that people who engage in a variety of experiences are more likely to retain positive emotions and minimize negative ones than people who have fewer experiences.[3]

Embrace the moment of stepping through new doors, where you'll find more opportunities inside. Count these new experiences as blessings because they open your eyes to a life you've yet to discover.

5

Live Simply

WE HAVE TO declutter our lives before we can focus on what is important to us.

When we live with so much abundance, it's hard to imagine a better experience with fewer choices. For every product we buy in a store or online, there is literarily a sea of options. Do we need all the selections? How often do you stare at the packaging of various products, unable to tell which one is the best for you? People call this decision paralysis. Too many options equal no option.

I used to work out at this boxing gym on my way to work before I transferred to a different hospital in another city. One morning after sweating buckets in their signature Triple Threat Workout, I was starving. I stopped by a cafe for my favorite avocado, ham, and egg sandwich and a fresh-squeezed orange juice. It wasn't until I took out my wallet that I realized I had only three dollars and some spare change left. The place only accepted cash. There wasn't enough time to go to another restaurant for breakfast. I apologized to the cashier and studied the menu for the cheapest item that could fill me up. Eventually, I settled on a whole wheat bagel with cream cheese. Driving to work, I ate the toasted bagel like it was the most delicious food in the world. It was crunchy and creamy. I felt the texture in my mouth; I noticed the subtle sweetness on my tongue. I felt happier with each bite I took. When I finished the bagel, I felt even better than on the days I had my favorite breakfast. You see, when my choices were taken away from me, I learned to appreciate more.

The same applies to life.

If you want an uncluttered mind, clean up your room. Get rid of the things you think you need but never use. Give them away; let your junk be someone else's treasure. If you can't decide what to keep, ask yourself what is meaningful to your life. Does this object serve your purpose? If not, send it to someone who will enjoy it. Giving makes us happier and gives us more control of our lives.

If particular online messages upset you each time you read them, unsubscribe, unfriend, or quit the group. Have a digital detox every Friday to reset your mental focus. You've been working hard all week; it's time to unwind with your life partner and kids. Don't spend hours staring at a screen that doesn't care if you're there. Tell your kids that they earn a quarter every time they catch you checking the phone on Fridays. They'll get the job done.

If you want a healthy and fit body, pay attention to what you eat and when you eat. Eat only when your body needs to refuel, not when you're stressed, bored, or sleepy as I did before. Pay attention to the texture, smell, and taste of your food, and chew slowly for proper digestion. Research shows slow eating makes you feel full sooner and curbs emotional eating. Connect with your meal. It's more intimate to you than your material possessions—you can't stuff your favorite photo down your throat, but the food you take in gets absorbed and becomes a part of you.

The more quality items you consume, the fewer toxins accumulate inside your body. That applies to medications as well. I study medicine for a living, but I don't take pills unless there's a clear therapeutic indication. Don't delay medical care because you don't want chemicals in your body. Treat your body when it needs help. What I want to discourage you from is unnecessary self-medicating behavior. I've talked to many health enthusiasts who take an excessive amount of "miracle" supplements for energy and health. If you are interested in quality research studies on the safety and efficacy of various complementary and alternative medicines, Nutritionfacts.org is a good resource. Chaired by Dr. Michael Greger, this organization provides strictly noncommercial, science-based public service on the latest in nutrition research via bite-sized videos.

Some of you may have the tendency to seek help from medications when you feel sad, unsatisfied, or low in energy. For example, you could experience insomnia, headache, and anxiety because you worry about being laid off from work. Your doctor may prescribe medications for you to treat such conditions, but they do nothing to the cause of your symptoms. As long as you continue worrying about your job, you'll experience these symptoms. So you go back to your doctor and get a higher dosage or more frequent treatment. Almost all medications carry adverse effects, ranging from mild gastrointestinal effects (such as nausea) to more serious central nervous system symptoms (such as memory loss). Mental stress often leads to physical pain, stiffness, and numbness. Relieving stress is the key to eliminate your symptoms, not pills.

Multiple research studies show physical activity improves mood and energy level, so go outside, take a walk, play basketball with your kids; take yourself out of that emotional dark corner. Once you calm down, evaluate if there's any evidence supporting your worry. In the example of a potential layoff, if you believe the outcome is likely, take action by looking for other job options. If you can't find anything within your field, try related work, or start your own business. Discuss with your life partner the possibilities of cutting back on spending. Teach your kids about the virtue of saving, and ask them to help you with the upcoming financial difficulty. It's never too early to teach children money management skills. We don't know who we are until we're challenged. There are many successful examples where people found a new calling when the old life shut the door on them. Remember, changes are often opportunities in disguise.

Some people carry this notion that you get what you pay for. Yes, a cheaper product may be inferior to its pricier counterpart in quality or performance. Luxury cars have a stronger road presence. Dressing in brand names improves your perceived status. If you can afford them, good for you. If you can't, there are things more meaningful to you than what meets the eyes. Price should not be the only criteria through which we measure our lives. Say you're invited to two parties on the same day. One is at an expensive venue filled with wealthy, beautiful people you've never met; the other is at your kid's school, where you get to see your son or daughter dressed up and put on a show for you. You're likely to go to the school party because it makes you feel proud, while the other makes you feel like a failure. Stop comparing to others. Everyone has a different story. You're the orange, and they're the apples.

Many good things in life are free. Love, friendship, and nature are all free and stand the test of time.

I grew up a city girl. I disliked camping in the wilderness, sometimes without a shower or toilet. It felt dirty and inconvenient. Chu loves camping in the woods, where we cook our meals outdoors, clean up in the river, and dig a hole for our human needs.

In the beginning, I complained a lot about the primitive lifestyle, but gradually my perception changed. I realized the beauty of living simply. I watched the brilliant sunrises in the woods and felt giddy over seeing the Milky Way in the night sky. I appreciated the hot drinks we made in the morning to warm up my achy body after sleeping on the ground. We saw all kinds of animals, big and small. As long as we left them alone, none of them bothered us. It was so peaceful and full of life in the forest. We got to witness the balance of nature at work, from plants to insects. Ethan learned how to skip stones expertly in a river. He enjoyed swimming in the open water while minding the safety concerns. We rode horses deep into the mountains where cars can't reach. We saw spectacular snow-capped mountains surrounding us in the peak of summer, where we were the only human to appreciate the view. These trips felt like a spiritual journey where my burden slowly fell away, and I was wholesome again.

Live simply. Make room for the magic moments in and around you.

6

Self-Therapy Against Anxiety, Guilt, and Shame

WE'RE ALL PRONE to and struggle with evil, energy-sucking emotions like anxiety, guilt, and shame. If you want a good life, you must keep those dark forces out of your head.

Men have the ability to compartmentalize emotions. They can laugh and have a beer right after a fistfight, while women still nurse their wounds six years after that hurtful comment overheard from inside the bathroom. The longer we hold onto these poisonous thoughts, the more incapable we are of feeling happy.

The simplest method of self-therapy against these emotions is writing about them on paper. Dr. James W. Pennebaker, chair of the psychology department at the University of Texas, Austin, has conducted much of the research on the health benefits of expressive writing.[4] He discovered writing about emotions may ease stress and trauma. When participants write nonstop while exploring their innermost thoughts and feelings without inhibition, it helps people to organize thoughts and give meaning to a traumatic experience. The process of writing may enable them to regulate their emotions and break free of the endless mental cycling typical of brooding or rumination. When people open up privately about a traumatic event, they are more likely to talk with others about it—and this suggests that writing leads indirectly to reaching out for social support that can aid healing. The next time you find yourself nursing the old wounds, write down your feeling in a notebook. Don't worry if you can only write words and phrases at first; no one can read it but you. Call it your journal of emotions. Create a habit of describing why you feel that way on paper, and date your entries. After a couple of months, go back and read your earlier writing; you'll see how far you've gone on the path of healing. Unleash your emotional burden on paper so you can live free.

Anxiety

The pressing desire to do better while believing you can't.

Having too many worries leads to anxiety. The emotion hits like a tornado or earthquake we are always underprepared for. Here I'll show you the temporary fix followed by a permanent solution.

Try this breathing exercise when you feel anxious. It takes less than a minute.

1. Close your mouth and inhale quietly through your nose to a mental count of four.
2. Hold your breath for a count of four.

3. Exhale through your mouth, making a whoosh sound to a count of four.
4. Hold your breath again for a count of four. This is one breath.
5. Inhale and repeat the cycle three more times.

Do you feel calmer now? Good. You just completed the tactical breathing exercise designed for Navy SEALs, SWAT teams, and police officers to remain calm in high-stress situations.[5] This technique breaks the moment of tension and allows oxygen to infuse your body to boost energy level. The next time you feel overwhelmed by stress, try this breathing technique to regain control. A research study by Nobel prize-winning researcher Elizabeth Blackburn shows a regular routine of mindful breathing or meditation strengthens genetic expression and even slows the natural process of aging.[6]

Let's move on to finding a permanent solution for your anxiety. The key is reverse engineering. *The Cambridge Dictionary* defines *reverse engineer* as the act of copying the product ... by looking carefully at how it is made.[7] This technique has been used widely in pharmaceutical, technology, and business industry.

To reverse engineer the best solution to a problem, we must start from the endpoint and work backward until we reach the starting point. This method keeps us laser-focused on our goal, preventing the unnecessary detours and unintentional backsteps. Once you grasp the concept, you can apply it to other issues at hand. This is very useful tool for planning and problems solving.

Think of a particular problem that keeps you up at night, and write it down at the bottom of a page in your notebook. Use as few words as possible to consolidate your thoughts.

This is your starting point. You want to be anxiety-free; that's your endpoint. Write STOP WORRYING ABOUT X PROBLEM on the top of the same page. Now, focus your mind on this question: If everything goes as you wish, what has to happen to relieve you from anxiety? Consolidate your thoughts into specific points, and record your wish list below the phrase STOP WORRYING ABOUT X PROBLEM. Next, brainstorm actions you can take to get you closer to that wish list. When you're done, record the steps you come up with.

Here's the example of how I dealt with anxiety over sudden infant death syndrome (SIDS). When my son, Ethan, was little, I was plagued with the fear that one morning I would walk up and find his plump cheeks icy cold. Everyone told me not to worry about it. But the nagging fear stayed with me every time I left his room. I woke up at random hours, checking on him, arranging and rearranging his blanket to minimize the risk of suffocation. This went on for months until one day I couldn't stand it anymore. I had to put an end to this ridiculous fear, or I would go crazy.

I wrote STOP THE UNREASONABLE FEAR ABOUT SIDS at the top of the page. Then I identified two things that could alleviate my anxiety.

1. *I can find a type of blanket that won't suffocate Ethan and still keep him warm and comfortable at night.*
2. *Ethan isn't at risk for stopping breathing on his own.*

Then I looked for options to get me closer to my wish list.

For item 1: *I could put Ethan in a sleep sack and remove his blanket.*

For item 2: *I looked up the information and statistics about SIDS and found Ethan wasn't at risk for spontaneous respiratory depression. Ethan's pediatrician assured me that as well.*

I posted the piece of paper on the wall. Every night, I would read it before tucking Ethan in, and I'd force myself to stay in bed when I habitually woke up in the middle of the night. I told myself if Ethan wasn't hungry or needed a diaper change, I shouldn't get up. After two weeks, my anxiety lessened. Soon, I cured my anxiety.

Guilt

The belief you are a terrible person because of the harm you imposed upon others, real and imagined.

We make mistakes, and we feel guilty for what we have done or what we believe we have done. It's normal to feel remorse after we mess up, but the constant inward blame is not.

Have you ever felt outraged by your child's accidental spill in the kitchen, or yelled at your partner for his inability to remember to buy milk? You were livid; your entire body shook over something so insignificant and forgivable. Ever wonder why you acted that way? Does stress make us scream at our loved ones?

Anger is often the outer manifestation of guilt. We defend our vulnerability by attacking people, and as a result, sink deeper into guilt afterward. Remember Helen from Chapter 3? She lashed out at her twin daughters even though she loves them dearly. The higher the standards we uphold, the harder we work and the easier it is to feel guilty for the things that go wrong. Sometimes, uncontrolled anxiety leads to guilt. In my case, if I hadn't overcome the fear of SIDS, I might have become chronically depressed, feeling guilty for the imagined harm I was causing my son. We have to forgive ourselves and turn the toxic energy into actions to make things better for ourselves and others.

Working moms often feel guilty about not spending enough time with their children. As long as the kids are safe and sound, your absence won't jeopardize their well-being. After all, most of us have to work to support our families. With child-rearing, what matters is the quality of time spent with them rather than the quantity. Because of the time restraints you have, focus on making your time together special and meaningful.

Before we tackle guilt, ask yourself if the harm you perceived actually happened or only exists in your head.

Factual Guilt

Say you had an argument with a friend. She rushed out, and a car hit her. She lost a leg and could no longer be a pro athlete. You hate yourself for the terrible thing you did to your friend. You could never face her again.

Write OVERCOMING YOUR GUILT at the top of a page. Now, let's examine the root cause of your guilt. It's hard to believe, but it's true that your action didn't cause the accident. It was her action (rushing out without looking) that led to the accident. Yes, she became angry and distracted because of your argument, but you're not in fact responsible for how disturbed she became. It's the same argument with driving on a stormy day. If a car spins on a freeway and runs into two other cars, can we blame the accident on the weather rather than the driver? In this case, your action only indirectly caused your friend harm. It's crucial to differentiate the direct and indirect cause.

Well, you say, the causal relation doesn't matter because your friend's life is ruined. She hates you, and you hate yourself. So we know the root cause of your guilt is that you fear your friend will never forgive you.

Let's reverse engineer the steps to get your friend to forgive you. To do this, you must start from the endpoint and work backward until you reach the starting point. There are many things you can do right away. Visit her and ask for her forgiveness. Offer to help to make her life more comfortable. Find out what other career options she is open to and find opportunities for her. Bring her to her favorite places and introduce her to new friends. If she's single, you might even help her meet her potential life partner. The bottom line is: don't get stuck in the dark corner with your debilitating thoughts while doing nothing to ease your friend's suffering.

You see, life goes on. She is young and healthy, and she bounces back faster than the average person. It's a pity that her pro career ended prematurely, but that's not the end of the world. She can still live a full life. You can too. Strengthen your friendship after the accident by giving back and helping her achieve the new goals in her life.

Self-Imposed Guilt

Don't feel guilty when you're luckier than those around you. Fate favors you, and it's not your fault. It's likely you're gifted and worked hard for what you have or accomplished, which led you on a path that few travel. Turn your burden into assets by helping those in need because of your unique position.

If you feel guilty because you're unable to meet everyone's needs, think of it this way: you can't help everyone every single time. It's impossible, even for a saint. Help when you can.

When you can't, say so. If people love you, they'll understand. If they abuse your kindness and guilt-trip you into doing more, then they don't care about you, so why should you kill yourself for them?

Maternal Guilt

Many moms experience guilt after yelling at their children when they're busy or tired. Helen from Chapter 3 did when helping her twins with their homework. I yelled when Ethan asked me at 8:45 p.m. on a Sunday to buy school supplies for his next morning's class. The image of him on the brink of tears flashed in front of my eyes as I drove to the nearest Target store to get the shopping done. I apologized to Ethan when I got home. We made a deal: I would try my best to be patient and supportive, and in the future he would tell me things like this ahead of time. Since then, I make it a rule to always apologize to Ethan for my impatience no matter how justifiable the situation may seem. Even though I'm an imperfect mom, I want Ethan to feel that he is the perfect child for me.

If your children rely on you for homework help, teach them problem-solving skills rather than solving each problem with them. It's their job to practice what they learn at school, and your job to assist, not to take over. Let your kids do the work themselves. If they ask for your help, try understanding what they struggle with first. Be sure to use their familiar methods to explain a new concept. This way, your children will likely build confidence to tackle harder problems by themselves in the future. Both self-reliance and confidence are important for a growing mind.

Tell your children you understand that learning new things are hard, and everyone makes mistakes. The first time my husband drove on the left side of the road in New Zealand, the windshield wipers turned on every time he tried to give a turn signal. Make sure your kids understand it's okay to fail as long as they learn from their mistakes.

Shame

The dark cloak you wear that no one else can see.

Everyone experiences shame. Together with vulnerability and insecurity, these acute emotions make us who we are. Shame can be related to our looks or to a part of our body; how we fail to succeed when we are expected to; how we suck at the one thing that comes easily for everyone else.

Dr. Brené Brown is a well-known researcher in guilt, shame, and vulnerability. She defines shame as "the intensely painful feeling or experience of believing we are flawed and therefore unworthy of acceptance and belonging."[8] The longer we keep shame to ourselves, the more powerful it becomes. The antidote, Brown says, is empathy. By talking about your shame with a friend who expresses empathy, the painful feeling will go away.

So open up to someone who wants you to be happy, who loves you even when you don't love yourself, who won't judge you despite knowing your secret.

Ethan and I had a conversation about shame when he was eight years old. He had just finished reading the novel *Wonder* by R. J. Palacio. It was a story about Auggie, a ten-year-old boy born with a rare facial deformity and a cleft lip, who gains confidence through friendships at a local private school. I asked Ethan if he would be a friend with someone like Auggie. He said he would because Auggie was a good person and very funny.

"What if you looked like Auggie, would you go to school and make friends?" I asked.

Ethan didn't answer me. When I asked him again, he said no, because he didn't want people to stare at him.

I told Ethan I would love him regardless of how he looked. "That's because you're my mommy. Other people won't."

"What if you are a good person and very funny?"

Ethan shook his head. "No. I would rather stay at home."

So I hugged him and told him what mattered was on the inside, not the outside. "When you make friends, make sure they are good people and very funny."

7

Self-Therapy Against Jealousy, Bitterness, and Meanness

WE EXPERIENCE JEALOUSY and bitterness more often than we admit, and these often lead to meanness. They're the seeds of our own dissatisfaction, seeking every opportunity to germinate and sprout out of the dark soil of the mind. Having fleeting bad thoughts is human. We only become ugly when we let the bad thoughts overpower the good ones.

Jealousy

The evil sister of admiration who swears vengeance.

Jealousy is the slow simmer of a bitter potion. The longer you drink from it, the more miserable you feel.

Ever met a gorgeous lady who possesses all the good fortunes in life, including a wealthy, loving husband, adorable kids, and a big house? She babbles on and on about her perfect life while the rest of us feel awful in comparison.

Like it or not, nothing is fair in life. Someone gets it all. Good for her, and leave it at that. If you only keep good thoughts in your head, luck may come your way too.

Don't compare, or it'll lead you to despair. Many things are out of your control, so don't waste your energy on them. Focus on the things you can change; the result will be so much more gratifying.

Every life has its own share of trials. What is glamorous on the outside isn't always the same on the inside. When you happen upon the shocking underside of some people's lives, you might never want to trade places with them.

The iconic actress and sex symbol Marilyn Monroe died childless and alone of a drug overdose at age thirty-six. She wrote in her book *My Story*, "Sometimes I've been to a party where no one spoke to me for a whole evening. The men, frightened by their wives or sweeties, would give me a wide berth. And the ladies would gang up in a corner to discuss my dangerous character."[9] I remember reading this passage and thinking to myself, "As much as I dream of being admired by the entire nation, I couldn't live with the disabling loneliness." Could you?

Have you ever thought about why we aren't jealous of the most famous people, even though they had the most beauty, wealth, and power? It's because our paths never crossed theirs. There's nothing in common between us—we didn't graduate from the same college, work in the same department, or have children who went to the same schools. We didn't start from the same reference point, so it doesn't matter how far they've gone ahead of us.

If you ever feel the potion of jealousy bubbling inside your chest, take a deep breath and count your blessings. Relive all the joyous moments of your life, the wonderful surprises you received, from present day all the way back to the freckle-faced boy in middle school who gave you his favorite comic book. Fill your mind with joy and gratitude until there's no more room for poisonous thoughts. Focus on the things you do well, the areas where you excel. You're perfect in your own imperfect ways. Remember that.

Bitterness and Meanness

The desperate attempt against life's unfairness.

The two ugly creatures of bitterness and meanness go hand in hand. It's hard to say which is worse. They are the two ends of one street; neither direction gets you anywhere. Bitterness and meanness are the result of a long history of disappointment, unresolved anger, and the need to take it out on others.

My advice is, don't go there. These emotions are poisonous bullets that shoot back at the one who pulls the trigger.

While working for airline executives years ago, I had a female coworker who went out of her way to make my work life difficult. Fresh out of college, I was naïve and idealistic, eager to prove myself. The more recognition I received at work, the meaner she treated me. Soon I heard the rumors she spread about me and felt alienated from the rest of the team. By then I realized the corporate world wasn't for me. I started attending evening classes for a master's degree. Looking back, I should thank her for pushing me to take action. I would never have done it if it weren't for her harsh treatment of me. After I left the job, I heard her bullying tactic backfired and she had to leave her position.

Don't let people suffer just because you are miserable. Karma works in mysterious ways. If you don't care about your own life, think about your children's. How would you feel if someone used the same nasty tactic on your precious darlings?

Help those in need if you can. If you can't, don't make things worse for them. The world is small. One day, you may find the table has turned, and you're ridiculed by someone you once mistreated. How would that feel?

Meanness and bitterness have a way of expressing them-selves on your face. People can spot that from a mile away. The good folks won't associate with you. One day, you'll wake up surrounded by your equally miserable friends.

Find a better way to spend your energy—self-improvement is a good start. Learn to be kind to yourself, and you'll be kind to others.

8

Don't Let Fear Stop You

DO YOU HAVE something you've always wanted to try but never get around to doing? What has stopped you from realizing your goal? Too much responsibilities and too little time? No, the real answer is fear.

Fear of the Unknown

Fear is like a locked door, keeping us safe with few opportunities.

We are all afraid of the unknown. The mysterious black hole of danger looms over our heads. We imagine all kinds of awful things that could happen. We say our lives aren't that bad, at least everything is familiar. That is one of the reasons an abused wife stays in the toxic relationship. That is also why some of us continue working day after day at the same job we hate.

Remember the first time you swam in the open water, feeling the wind, the current, that vast body of water around you and beneath you? It was so scary. There was no plastic divider to define the lanes, no walls you could hold onto. Once you relaxed, you realized no matter how deep the water was, you would stay afloat as you had learned in the pool.

All good things require risk-taking—going for a job interview you have little experience in, taking on a big project at work, letting your kids go to school by themselves for the first time. Every milestone in your life requires risk-taking, and the bolder you are, the more you achieve. Unlock the door of fear and you'll realize there's nothing to be afraid of. You become more confident of your abilities as you push open more doors that lead you to success.

Here is my story of fear. For years I skied on the green runs for beginners, while my husband, Chu, and my son, Ethan, skied on the advanced runs. The green runs were easy for me. I knew every bump and turn so well I could ski with my eyes closed. Whenever Chu proposed I join them on the advanced runs, I would always decline because I wasn't ready. Meanwhile, by the time Ethan turned nine he had become a double black diamond skier. Chu was a good teacher, and Ethan was fearless, so naturally he progressed to an expert level within a few short years.

One day, Chu brought me over to a lift I had never seen before. Snow covered everything, including the signage, thanks to a white-out storm the day before. I knew it wasn't a beginner run as I examined the steep slope beneath me.

"Just push off and go. It's not much steeper than the green runs," Chu urged me.

His explanation didn't help. The image of my skis flying in different directions flashed in front of my eyes. The more I thought about the perils of going down that slope, the more paralyzed my legs became.

"I can't," I told him. It was cold at the top of the mountain. The wind cut into my face like blades.

"Ethan's down there waiting. We have to go," Chu said.

"You go and find him," I said, "I'll be fine."

"Don't take too long. It's freezing up here," Chu said before gliding downhill. Easy-peasy.

I stood still, watching people push off, their colorful ski jackets getting smaller by the second. My feet felt numb. I thought about how exhilarating it would be to meet Chu and Ethan at the bottom of the hill and tell them I did it. I thought about going down by the lift of shame, avoiding people's eyes as I rode closer to the lift station where long lines of people waited to get on. I didn't want to be a failure, but I was scared.

I asked myself what was the worst thing that could happen if I skied down. A thick coat of powder snow blanketed everything underneath. If I fell, it wouldn't hurt. Also, I knew how to stop myself from going too fast on the slope, so it was unlikely that I would fall. Finally, I asked myself this question: "When was the last time I did something I was proud of?"

I couldn't think of any. By then, my feet were so numb I knew I had to move. I bit my frozen lip and pushed off. The wind was merciless. The speed was much faster than what I was used to. Subconsciously, I leaned backward, which made me go even faster. I felt the bottom of my skies bouncing off the bumps on the slope. I was losing control.

Chu had always told me the steeper the slope, the more I needed to lean forward and put pressure on the front of the skis. Remembering his words, I shifted forward, pressing my sheens against the tongue of my boots. Immediately, I had better control of my skis. I bent down further to make my turns smooth. About halfway down the slope, I got into a rhythm that felt so good. I realized how exhilarating it was to ski on an advanced run with all the added speed and difficulty. I have never gone back to the beginner runs since.

You see, I never knew I was ready until I pushed off on that intimidating slope. We all need to take calculated risks to stretch our potentials and reach for higher goals.

The wisdom of adulthood teaches us to be cautious and suspicious. But not all unknowns are dangerous. Without trying, we'll never know if something could work out. Do you know most Americans die regretting not doing the things they wished they had done? Don't let it be you.

The interesting thing about fear is that once you get over one fear, other fears fade away as well. It's all in our head, ladies.

Remember Nike's slogan: *Just Do It.*

Fear of Failure

Failure doesn't mean we're not good enough, not smart enough.

Failure is circumstantial. It has nothing to do with your talent or value as a person. Here are four tips for avoiding fear of failure.

1. **Learn to put things in perspective.** Stop dwelling on how miserable you feel and focus on what went wrong

and how you can best rectify the situation. Take the emotion out of the equation of success.

2. **Learn to think like men.** They have the innate ability to put the sting of failure behind them and jump right back into action. I attended the Association of Writers and Writing Programs (AWP) conference in Oregon in spring 2019. There was a panel of editors at the most prestigious literary magazines in the country. They all said the same thing. When they receive a submission they like but it doesn't fit for their upcoming issue, they will often ask the writer to submit again for future consideration. Nine out of ten times, the male writers send in their work for the very next publication. Female writers, however, are often never heard from again.

3. **Failure is an opportunity to look for new ways to improve your odds of winning.**

4. **Success depends on many factors: timing, people, location, and approach.** All of these components have to work together. If you failed, analyze each of these elements and figure out exactly where things went wrong, then correct them and try again. If you still fail, go through the same process until you get it right. Knowledge is what we learn from others; wisdom is the ability to use that knowledge to achieve our goals. Nothing beats the satisfaction of finally figuring out how to become good at something after multiple failures. Begin building your wisdom today, and teach your children to do the same. They'll learn much more from failure than success.

9

Water and Sunshine for Your Love

HOW MUCH QUALITY time do you spend with your partner every day?

For most of us, it is less than thirty minutes a day. Some moms confess "None." They don't have time for one-on-one. The kids and the house suck up all their energy and time. How can they relax and talk when there are loads of work to do at home? When they finally have a moment to sit down and catch a breath, they spend it watching TV or on Facebook. They put their most important relationship at the bottom of the priority list, below grocery shopping, cat videos, and *Game of Thrones*.

You can't sustain love without spending quality time together.

Think of love as a flower. With water and sunshine, it blooms in the most spectacular color. When in love, you were blooming. You wanted every minute of the day to be with each other. After the kids, you water the relationship less and less. Without sunshine, you let your appearance go. When problems arise, you blame each other, saying hurtful words over trivial things. The flower withers, and you become cohabiting neighbors. You stop feeling each other while sharing the same bed. One day, someone else who's keen on water and sunshine will steal one of you away, leaving a broken family behind.

If you want a happy relationship, ask yourself how often you water the flower of your love? When was the last time you laughed with each other, doing the activities you used to enjoy together? If you find yellowing leaves, rekindle the love with intimacy and care. Remember the happiness circles we talked about in Chapter 1? A loving relationship is an essential part of your well-being. Don't kill the precious flower.

Motivational speaker Tony Robbins writes about the five disciplines of love on his website.[10] In a nutshell, here's his advice:

1. Stop focusing on yourself, focus on your partner's love and needs.
2. Tell the truth. The more vulnerable you are, the more power you have.
3. Always think about the positive intent. Don't play the blame game. Apologize when you're wrong.
4. Praise your loved one specifically for what he has done for you.
5. Learn to forgive and forget. It's better to be in love than to be right.

Can you learn from his advice?

When I first met Nora, she told me the only reason she stayed in the marriage was for her kids. She married her husband for love, but he quickly changed after the kids were born. He worked long hours. Even when he was home, he was uninterested in helping her with the chores. When she complained about having to do everything by herself, he told her it was because she always criticized him for not doing things the right way. She had tears in her eyes when she told me this: "I caught him watching porn while I was scrubbing the kitchen floor." After the incident, she couldn't sleep for days, wondering how their marriage had broken down so fast.

I asked if they ever talked about the incident, and she told me there was nothing left to talk about.

"It's over between us," she said.

"Do your kids love him?" I asked.

"They do," she said with a sigh. "He buys them their favorite junk food and takes them to play outside."

"So he cares about the kids," I said.

"I told him not to buy the unhealthy stuff for them, but he just won't listen."

"Does he eat junk food himself?"

She nodded. "I give up on changing his diet. He'll never change."

"When you two were dating, did it bother you that he had an unhealthy eating habit?"

She shook her head. "He was adventurous, hilarious too, cracked me up all the time. It was so much fun being with him, I never cared about his diet."

"But it bothers you now."

"Well, I have to think about what is good for the kids. I'm responsible for their future."

"Has he ever asked you to change?" I asked.

She blinked at the question. "What do you mean? I prepare homemade lunches for the kids. I help them with their homework every day. Never missed a single PTA meeting. I do everything I need to do."

"How often do you talk to your husband?" I asked. "Not about the kids and the day-to-day things."

She considered the question.

"When was the last time you asked him how he felt? What does he expect from you?"

She pursed her lips. "Well, he looks okay to me. I'm the one who's suffering, not him."

"If you don't mind me asking," I continued, "when was the last time you had sex with him?"

She stared at me. "I'm always so tired, you know?"

I told her to go home and schedule some intimate time with her husband. Once she felt comfortable enough to talk about the incident, she should be honest about her feelings of being betrayed. When she came back to see me in two weeks, she looked happier. I noticed she had a haircut that made her look younger. When I complimented her, she told me they had a long talk after sex. She realized she had been unintentionally driving him away with her complaints and criticism. He loved her but felt resentful when she picked on him all the time. He craved the passion they once shared, and the porn was a poor substitute for her lack of interest in intimacy. Six months later, when I saw her again, she told me happily that her husband has finally adapted to a healthier diet after abnormal cholesterol test results. She began to praise him for each little step he took toward that positive change. The last time I heard they'd started going to the gym together.

This is one example of how water and sunshine keep your love strong. The next time you encounter problems with your relationship, ask yourself if you have neglected your partner's feelings and needs, and how you can apply the five disciplines of love to resolve the issues.

10

Raising Resilient, Responsible, and Resourceful Kids

WE ALL WANT the best for our children, but have we provided them with what they need for success?

In June 2019, I polled an entrepreneur group on Facebook with this question: *What is the one thing you wish your parents taught you?* Out of the ninety-eight responses I received, 36 percent wished they had learned money management, 35 percent self-confidence, and 20 percent love and support.[11]

There are many schools of thought in terms of the best parenting approach. I group them roughly into two camps: The Tiger Mom (Eastern) camp believes discipline and strong work habits are the keys to success. The name comes from the book *Battle Hymn of the Tiger Mother* by Amy Chua, a Yale law school professor.[12] The Western approach, which I've dubbed the Free-Range Mom camp, values individuality and support for children's well-being.

I like the structured child-rearing from the Tiger Mom camp, and the supportive element from the Free-Range Mom camp, so I came up with a hybrid mothering method, the Experiential Nurturing model. The idea is to allow children to build confidence and character by developing problem-solving skills and critical thinking through life experiences. The goal of this model is to teach children to be the 3 R's—resilient, responsible, and resourceful.

Most new moms stress over their children's physical growth and development milestones during the early years. Pay special attention to your kids' personalities and preferences. Notice what types of activities get them excited, and what tires them easily. Are they adventurous or cautious? Do they enjoy books and stories or prefer working with their hands? Instead of correcting their natural inclinations to fit your preference or making them act like their siblings, identify their positive traits and provide relevant experience to further develop their interests and skills. The Experiential Nurturing model focuses on creating opportunities to support children's natural talents while allowing them to learn independently to build confidence and resilience.

As I mentioned in Chapter 2, our job is to figure out how to maximize the effect of our strengths while not letting our weaknesses stop us. As parents, we need to do the same for our children. When they grow up, they'll have the knowledge and courage to compete in the real world.

Through research on the indicators for long-term success, I found two characteristics crucial in child development: curiosity and grit.

Curiosity

The Cambridge Dictionary defines *curiosity* as an eager desire to know or learn about something.[13] I associate curiosity with open-mindedness, innovation, high adaptation, optimism, and respect.[14]

To nurture my son's curious mind, I provided two primary experiences when he was little: reading and traveling.

Reading—To See the World through Words

Reading not only helps children with cognitive functions such as creativity and imagination, but it also helps them discover their interests so parents can facilitate their growth.

I started reading books to Ethan when he was about four months old. By then, he could move his little fingers on the board books and babble after me. Looking back, it was just as beneficial for me as for him. After a long day at school, the best relaxation for me was to be silly with him, talking in funny voices, and watch his facial expressions change as the animal characters went through their adventures.

I read to Ethan every day until he could read on his own. Still, he enjoyed snuggling up to me and reading the pages while I continued to perfect my vocal abilities. By the time he turned seven, I had borrowed for him the middle-grade books on the *New York Times* bestseller list from the local library. By age ten, he had finished reading *The Da Vinci Code* by Dan Brown. Although there were many words he didn't understand, he enjoyed the story.

When he was in fifth grade, I shared my reading list with him, which ranged from Pulitzer Prize-winning novels such as *All the Light We Cannot See* by Anthony Doerr and *Montana*

1948 by Larry Watson to nonfiction books in neurobehavioral science, business management, memoirs, wilderness and survival. Gradually, I recognized his interest in philosophy and neurobehavioral science. To support his newfound interest, I searched for the best books to further his learning on the subjects. When we attend parties or gatherings, our friends are often surprised by Ethan's depth of knowledge and unique perspective.

Traveling—To See How Big the World Is, Yet How Similar People Are

Bring your children to places to further their learning and understanding. Travel as far as you can so their eager eyes can witness the differences in nature and culture.

Don't just bring your kids to the theme parks for thrill rides and overpriced food. Yes, it's fun, but they learn little at those places. For the moms holding season tickets to Disneyland or Disney World, think again for your children's future. Many great sights are free to visit and offer so much more for young minds to explore.

Chu and I have taken Ethan overseas every year since he was four years old. We've been to many countries in Europe, Asia, Australia/Oceania, and America. Next, we want to visit Africa. We want to learn with him about the world.

If you can't afford to travel overseas, travel domestically. Take a road trip, and talk to each other on the long drive to ask questions and receive answers. My favorite road trip was to Yellowstone National Park in 2010. We drove from San Francisco to Jackson Hole in two days, passed by the glaciated landscape of Yosemite National Park, enjoyed the Mormon Tabernacle Choir in Salt Lake City, and watched rodeo in Cody, Wyoming.

Once we reached the park, we camped inside for seven nights, each day hiking different trails and teaching Ethan about nature preservation. Chu taught Ethan the science behind geothermal effect when we admired the majestic Old Faithful geyser that has erupted about every ninety minutes since 2000.[15] We watched a mother bear going grocery shopping in the woods with her cubs; we found reindeer behind our tent when we took photos of the spectacular sunrise; we saw a herd of bison cross the road in front of our SUV and were in awe of their massive size and bloodshot eyes; we saw beautiful wildflowers blooming in the valley where creeks ran free, and those giant trees whose names Ethan had to look up on the computer once we returned home.

Grit

The second characteristic crucial in child development is grit. *The Cambridge Dictionary* defines *grit* as bravery and strength of character. I associate grit with conscientiousness, resilience, and courage.

Many remarkable people in this world succeed not because of their exceptional talents but because of their reactions to challenges and adversities. They push on in the headwind, not letting self-pity and excuses stop them. To build your children's confidence, stamina, and tenacity, you must provide them the experiences centered on developing these positive traits. Build your children's characters when they are young. You can start with these five areas:

1. Coping skills
2. Practical life skills
3. Money management
4. Working/internship
5. Extracurricular activities

Coping Skills

When your children are little, encourage them to try new things. When they get frustrated, instead of stepping in and solving problems for them, help them analyze the situations and come up with their own solutions. Let your kids know no one can be good at everything, but everyone is good at something. Help them recognize and amplify their strengths through trial and error. Tell them not to compare to others because everyone is different.

Some kids have self-esteem issues, frequently the result of failing to meet their parents' high expectations. Eager parents set extremely high standards for their kids, leaving no room for errors. When children can't keep up with the demand, they believe they're a total failure. In just the first three months of 2019, two students committed suicide at Stanford University because of the mounting pressure to do well.[16] What a tragedy, which could be prevented by infusing kids with the right message when they were young: no one is perfect. Their best is good enough.

Not doing well in school doesn't necessarily mean there's no future for the academically challenged. If your kids struggle with school despite genuine effort to learn, maybe traditional education isn't for them. Instead of forcing them to enter college, consider a trade school where a hands-on occupation might suit them better. Countless self-made millionaires had no formal education; their will to succeed and ability to adapt make their achievement possible.

You can create small challenges to help your children build confidence and resilience. Allow your sons and daughters opportunities to be proud of overcoming something themselves.

When my family traveled in France in late 2008, we heard the news that Barack Obama had won the presidential election. That day, we took Ethan to the iconic Eiffel Tower. We asked Ethan if he would like to climb the 704 steps with us to the second-floor viewpoint. Only the strongest kid could do it, I told him. He was eager to prove his strength. We set out climbing. I held his hand, and we went up slowly with frequent breaks. While we rested at about halfway, a young man and his girlfriend saw us. The young man told the girlfriend if a four-year-old could do it, she could too. Ethan was so proud of himself after we arrived at the top. This experience must have boosted his self-confidence. Before the trip, he mostly spoke phrases; after the trip, he told stories in complete sentences with plenty of made-up words to enhance his speech. The transformation delighted us.

Now that Ethan is a teenager, he wants to bulk up his muscles. About eight months ago, he decided to do 200 pushups a day to build his chest and back muscles. After three months, Ethan increased the number to 300 a day. By this rate, he said, he would reach a million pushups in nine years. So far, he has kept his promise, even on the days he is sick. I admire his grit. I'm proud of providing a good foundation for his goal-oriented mindset.

Practical Life Skills

While technology brings us efficiency and convenience, it takes away the opportunities to learn life skills. Texting short, abbreviated phrases to each other trumps face-to-face conversations. Food deliveries through smartphone apps beats cooking at home. The more advanced technology is, the more dependent we become. It isn't difficult to imagine that in a global energy crisis or the breakdown of the internet network, few will know how to function and survive.

One mom told me that her son at college in Hawaii called to ask her how to unclog his toilet with a plunger. It sounds like a joke, but it isn't funny. Basic life skills such as cleaning up after oneself, doing laundry, making simple repairs at home teach kids responsibility, discipline, and independence.

During our frequent camping trips, we often ask Ethan to help prepare easy and delicious meals with natural ingredients. He has a group of friends he knew since kindergarten. Ethan has made beef kebabs for their beach cookouts, organized trips to various museums, and hiked in city parks.

Money Management

American education is insufficient in money management. Even some adults struggle with financial terms such as compound interest. It's important to have age-appropriate money talks with children. Moms can help kids understand the value of healthy spending based on the calculation of return on investment. Exposing children to books on money management for kids is a good start. It's also important to explain to them the process of decision making for big-ticket items in the house.

On our overseas trips, we give Ethan an allowance for him to manage and ask him to take charge of grocery shopping. When in Norway, he was the one to select which items to buy for maximum value, paid for them, and made sure the change was correct. If you want your kids to grow up smart, responsible, and independent, start training them early. While people say it's never too late to learn new skills, well, I say it's never too early to learn either.

Two years ago, my husband Chu and I opened a custodial brokerage account for Ethan using his savings. Ethan's job was to read the earnings report and analyze the industry trend. We introduced him to Warren Buffett's investment strategies. Chu helped him decide the goal of his portfolio and the level of risk tolerance most fitting for his age and assets. We want Ethan to acquire financial planning skills by thinking long-term. Sometimes, Ethan gets hung up on the down-trending of his stocks. He complains how many cars he had to wash to get the money he lost. We told him not to worry about the temporary market fluctuations. Investment is a long game; always focus on the end result.

Working/Internship

Kids don't truly understand the value of money until they have earned it themselves. Instead of telling kids to focus on schoolwork all the time, ask them to take up age-appropriate jobs to practice real-life skills.

At age twelve, Ethan asked his older cousins if they would like him to wash their cars for ten dollars each. Everyone said yes, and Ethan did a fantastic job of making their vehicles shine. He saved the money for his stock account. This past summer, he just finished his first paid internship at the San Francisco Police Department through a youth development program. He was so proud to receive his very first paycheck in the mail! Many cities have such programs introducing teens to various job opportunities. Check out your children's school website, local public libraries, or city government website for information on internship and application requirement.

Extracurricular Activities

Do children need to learn to play a musical instrument or a sport, or join the robotics team? More and more kids burn out doing various activities assigned by their well-intentioned parents. You should include children in the discussion about which activities are necessary and which are not. Not that you should let kids call the shots. Find the activities that best fit their strengths, and present your children with options to choose from. Using this supervised autonomy approach, kids are more likely to enjoy their activities rather than simply going through the motions.

In Amy Chua's memoir, she shares that her older daughter, Sophia, made her piano debut at Carnegie Hall at age fourteen. Amy instilled strict rules for structuring Sophia's life around piano training. I admire Sophia's extraordinary musical achievement, but I can't embrace Amy's parenting approach. I introduced Ethan to the piano when he was six. He told me he hated it after a year. I stopped the piano lessons. A few years later, he picked up the violin on his own, practicing often with no one asking. I thought violin would be the go-to instrument for his musical expression. Last year, he switched to a guitar. As a mom, I can't predict or dictate what he likes and how he wants to live his life. My job is to provide guidance and support when he needs help to pursue his areas of interest.

Spend quality time with your children. Instead of cramming their lives with activities they don't care for, talk to them and listen to their concerns. Be there when they need you, and step aside when they want to be independent. Before long, kids will move away from home to a new city and start a new life. The deep bond between you and your children is worth so much more than the long list of activities they can put on their resume.

I know you have to work, and there are always tons of things to do around the house, but stop what you are doing and listen to your children when they wish to talk. Let them know you'll never judge them or force them to be somebody else. Be patient with them. Allow them to learn at their own pace.

Space for Teens

Being a teenager is a sensitive and confusing time. These not-still-children-but-not-yet-adults try to figure out who they are and what they want to do with their lives. Moms often feel anxious over the sudden emotional detachment of their once sweet *babies*. Allow teens the time and space to sort out the confusion and handle peer pressure. The more you respect their individuality, the more respectful they will become. Being inquisitive and spying on your children will damage the trust between you and push them farther away. Think about your own teenage years, how you resented anyone invading your space. We were in their shoes only a few decades ago. We thought our parents knew nothing and we knew everything.

There will be moments they want to talk about the things they can't figure out on their own. Listen carefully to what worries them before jumping to conclusions and criticizing them. Use those opportunities to show them how much you love them and want to help them do well.

Ethan is now at the age where he gives only one- or two-word answers to my questions. He has more words for his friends. So I just ask if I can hug him. When we hug, I always tell him I love him. I'll say, "Whenever you need me, just say it," to which he always replies, "I will."

Yesterday, I took Ethan to see his pediatrician for a well-child checkup. We had a good conversation on our way there. I told him if he had concerns about his body, he could discuss them with his doctor, and I would step out. Waiting in the hallway, I kept myself busy answering emails. Ten minutes later, the exam room door was still closed. I wondered if there was something serious that Ethan had kept from me. He must have read my face when he finally came out of the room. "No worries," he said with a shy smile, "Everything is fine."

Don't worry if you've done little to nurture your children's creativity and grit. Start now by reading to them or with them. Take them to places they haven't been to. Build a connection with your children as soon as you can. Give them small challenges to build confidence. Teach them life skills that will benefit them for the rest of their lives. Improve their financial literacy. Encourage them to take up age-appropriate jobs to understand the value of money. Include them in the discussion about extracurricular activity arrangements. Respect their space when they need it. Be emotionally available when they need reassurance, encouragement, and a healthy dose of praise. If your parents have been your role models, carry on the same role to your children. If they haven't been, be the parent you wish you had when you were young.

Don't feel guilty about what you haven't done. As long as you love your children and communicate that love, they'll know. Children are incredibly curious and forgiving. Your love and understanding will make a world of difference in their lives. They'll think of you when they teach their own children.

Love your children by giving them the opportunities to learn and be the 3 R's—resilient, responsible, and resourceful.

THE BODY

Your body is your power house.
Feed it the purest fuel, award it the kindest upkeep.
Rest and recharge so it can take you anywhere your mind desires.
Your beauty is your inner strengths shining through the body you love and care for.

11

Full Body Awareness

ON THE WEBSITE of the National Organization for Women (NOW), I found the following statistics:[17]

- 40–60 percent of elementary school girls are concerned about their weight.
- At age thirteen, 53 percent of American girls are "unhappy with their bodies."
- This grows to 78 percent by the time girls reach age seventeen.
- 45.5 percent of teens report considering cosmetic surgery; 43.7 percent of women over age sixty report considering cosmetic surgery.

Why aren't we happy with our bodies? The reasons are deeply rooted in our beliefs.

First, we believe there's a golden standard for feminine beauty ideal. If we don't meet the criteria, we aren't attractive.

In middle school, the prettiest girl on campus was the image of an ideal body. As we grow, we see more and more gorgeous celebrities in mass media to confirm the belief.

If beauty can come with different skin tones, hair, and eye colors, why can't it be in different sizes? I'm only five feet three inches tall. Standing next to the tall and slim Kendall Jenner (my niece's biggest idol), I'd look like a dwarf.

I had reached my full height by age eleven. Back then, I was the first girl in our class to have round breasts. I tried to cover them up because the other girls were all flat-chested. I wanted to be just like them. It was especially inconvenient to compete in the 100-meter dash with two watermelons hanging on my chest.

I have a naturally small waist. Childbirth made my hips grow wider, so as a result, I now have an hourglass figure. I make sure I dress in the way that accentuates my feature.

Second, we like to compare. Imagine you are invited to a party where you don't know anyone other than the host. What's the first thing you do when you arrive? You look around and analyze the people you see. Are they better looking, younger, dressed nicer? The more attractive they look, the more miserable you feel about yourself.

My husband once brought me to a party where we were obviously underdressed. The people were friendly, but I felt self-conscious the whole time. My husband, though, didn't seem to notice anything. He cracked jokes with strangers and had a great time. When we drove home, I asked him why he wasn't concerned that we weren't as dressed up as others. "Why?" he said. "It's not like we intended to upset anyone. They misinformed me. Don't keep thinking about yourself.

Focus on other people, get them to talk about themselves, and you'll blend in well."

Third, we believe we can't be beautiful if our bodies are flawed. Do you know even supermodels have insecurities? Check out the TED Talk by supermodel Cameron Russell.[18] You'll learn that as gorgeous as the runway stars are, they are the most insecure people on the planet. No one is perfect, indeed.

Enough with the serious soul searching; now let's do a total body scan.

Find the biggest mirror you have at home and strip naked when no one is around. Examine your whole body as if you are seeing it for the first time. Stopping staring at the body parts you hate the most. Inspect the areas you have paid little attention to for years. Run your fingers on those parts of your skin and take in how different your touch feels. Instead of picking on your flaws, identify the areas that look good to you. Maybe you have toned arms, shapely legs, a firm butt, or full breasts. Think of ways to make them look better with flattering clothes. A properly fitted bra will magically lift your assets while tricking the eyes into believing you have a smaller waist. If you're happy with your neckline, wear a little V neck with a necklace that compliments your eye color. Suddenly you look sophisticated and charming.

I have masculine calves. For years I hated them, and I never wore skirts during my younger years. One day, a woman on the street commented on how nice my calves looked. I was shocked. When I realized her compliment was genuine, I realized how ridiculous I had been about my body. Even though I still can't fit into most of the knee-high boots, I bought the wide-calved ones online. Now I wear dresses almost every day. It has become my signature style.

Remember what I said in Chapter 2: it's much more satisfying and effective to enhance our strengths than to improve our weaknesses. The same principle applies to your body. Give love to the parts of your body you have neglected for so long. Learn to look for beauty within you and make it shine. We are all beautiful in our own ways. It's time to switch the lens we have been looking through.

Pay attention to how you walk. Is your back straight, eyes looking ahead? Are your shoulders relaxed or scrunched up? Are you dragging your feet as you walk as if you're carrying an invisible load on your back? Examine the bottoms of your shoes to see how uneven your steps are. Learn to stand up; your body deserves a proper posture. When you stand up straight, you'll look taller and slimmer, and even breathe better.

Inspect your skin. If it's dry and rough, consider applying body lotion every day right after the shower while the skin is still moist. Within a week, you'll notice how much softer and smoother your skin becomes.

Stop wearing ill-fitted clothes and shoes. Don't age your body beyond your years. If you see the grooves on top of your shoulders, you've been wearing bras too small for you. Get measured the next time you go shopping. You'll look so much better with a well-fitted undergarment. All the unsightly bulges your old bra created will disappear immediately. Talk about an instant transformation.

There's More to Beauty than Your Looks

The way you look on the outside is only part of what makes you beautiful. Pay attention to your unhealthy eating habits. Stop abusing your body with all the chemicals from drug use, chain-smoking, and excessive drinking. When I took anatomy class in graduate school, I saw a man who had died of lung cancer. His lungs looked like a charred cardboard box, filled with scar tissues and holes. It was a horrific sight. Don't wait until you have to tow an oxygen tank around before you consider quitting.

If you rely on chemicals for your emotional relief, realize they're not the permanent fix. Masking your feelings doesn't make problems go away. Tackle the root cause of your problem instead. It takes courage, and it takes time. Be strong for your kids. What you do to yourself affects how they treat themselves. Think of their future and make the right choice. You want to live a long and healthy life to meet your grandchildren, even your great-grandchildren.

Before you do anything to your body, think about the long run. How could it affect you twenty, thirty years down the road? Does it align with your values, or is it just a way to express your frustration? We all live through difficulties in life. It's what we do that makes us who we are. Think about the person you always wanted to be and act as if you were that person. Life is easier if you focus on making the right choice each day.

12

The Battle Against Nature

MY MOM HAS a stack of photos she doesn't like. Either her hair looks funny or the shots weren't flattering. Every few years or so, she examines her stack and returns some of the old photos back to her photo albums. She'll say, "Gosh, I looked so much younger then."

Our bodies are at the mercy of gravity and time. Similar to the tectonic plates shifting on this planet, we observe large-scale changes in ourselves—hills become valleys and basins rise to be mountains. Fat finds a home at the most unwanted places. Even if you work out regularly, the trouble areas are too stubborn to leave. Slower metabolism caused by aging forces you to ration how much of your favorite foods you can eat. When younger, you could eat pizza for dinner and still look great. Now you feel your waistline expand right after indulging in an ice cream waffle cone.

Time is unkind. New wrinkles show up without an invitation as your worries continually pop up. Somewhere between rush hour traffic and housework, your skin loses its youthful glow and suppleness. Some of you may sigh, admit prime time is over, and go on with your lives. The truth is, everyone gets old one day.

Some of you might be alarmed by the sudden signs of aging and rush to get the most effective rejuvenating regimen or procedures. Every few months, you would find new imperfections and repeat the cycle. There's only one life to live, you believe.

Aging is not all bad. Most people like aged cheese, wine, and meats. They erupt in your mouth with sophisticated flavors and textures, make you feel like falling in love again. With maturity comes the wisdom and elegance that youngsters can't imitate. Instead of striving to be young forever or letting go of our appearances, why don't we aim for looking younger than our ages?

Do the following exercise with me in front of a mirror:

Start by standing up straight, shoulders back and relaxed, focus on your eyes in the mirror. Take a deep breath through your nose and hold it for a count of four. Exhale through your mouth to a count of four. Think about the happiest moments in your life and give yourself a big smile. Say aloud and with conviction, "I'm grateful for what I have."

Notice you look more youthful in the mirror than you did just a minute ago? You look younger because you are calm, grateful, and happy. When we brood over losses, they are all we see; when we count our blessings, luck will come our way. Do this exercise every day to remind yourself you have a life worth living.

Aging Gracefully

Graceful aging only requires six things, most of which are free:

1. Maintain a good posture
2. Have a good night's sleep
3. Get active
4. Stay hydrated
5. Adopt a skincare routine
6. Be grateful

Let's look at each of these in detail.

Maintain a Good Posture

The correct posture helps to ease low back pain and relieve neck and shoulder tension. In return, you'll increase lung capacity, improve circulation and digestion, improve core strength and energy level, reduce joint pain, and have fewer headaches. You'll not only look taller and thinner but also appear more confident. Just by standing up straight and making good eye contact, you give off the impression of intelligence and capability. If you tend to slouch, use a concealable posture corrector to help you form a good habit.

When you walk, your body should remain straight, eyes forward and shoulders back. Don't stomp or drag your feet. Walk with ease, lift one foot, touch down then switch legs at a rhythm.

If you want to appear youthful, add a bit of bounce to your steps. Have you ever watched teenagers walk down the street? They have so much rebound in their gaits, it's as if there are energy bunny batteries in their sneakers.

You'll find some great exercises with videos that will help you improve your posture at https://www.healthline.com/health/fitness-exercise/posture-benefits.[19]

Have a Good Night's Sleep.

When we're tired, we crave not just more food but also those that are higher in fat, sugar, and salt—foods we know are bad for us but which we are evolutionarily primed to love.[20] If your children or duties have been keeping you up at night, try to catch a nap during your lunch hour. Even a fifteen-minute shuteye will help improve your brain function and productivity. Sleep-deprived brains do a poor job of regulating appetite and impulses. If you're someone who has difficulty falling asleep or wakes up in the middle of the night, try this method used by the U.S. Navy to help soldiers fall asleep in two minutes. You'll wake up feeling better than if you take insomnia medications. The following is an abbreviated transcription of the instructions from a Bright Side video:[21]

- "Step One: Lie face up in bed. Relax your facial muscles, including your tongue, jaw, and the muscles around your eyes. If you realize you have a frown, focus on releasing the area in the center of your forehead. ..."
- "Step Two: Drop your shoulders as low as possible. This will also help you stretch and release the tension in your neck. Relax your upper and lower arm on one side, and then try it with the other arm."
- "Step Three: Breathe out and relax your chest. Feel your lungs fill up with air."
- "Step Four: Relax your legs. Release the tension from your thighs first and then let the relaxation travel down to your calves. Finally, focus on your feet and ankles."

- "Step Five: Now that the muscles in your body are relaxed, it's time to clear your mind completely. ... Imagine yourself lying in a canoe on a calm lake with nothing but a clear blue sky above you, ... [or lying] in a black velvet hammock in a pitch-black room. If these images don't work for you, tell yourself, 'Don't think, don't think, don't think' for about ten seconds."

The technique is said to work for a whopping 96 percent of people after six weeks of practice. So if you can't relax into sleep during the first couple of weeks, your mind is likely occupied with worries and the million things you have to do. Learn to focus on yourself, your breaths, how each part of your body feels as you slowly sink into the mattress. Keep practicing the method until you can turn off the noise in your head like a switch.

Get Active

Human bodies are not meant to sit all day. Inactivity leads to pain and inflammation because of reduced blood circulation. If you work at a desk, take a break and go outside; enjoy the breeze and fresh air. Walk around the building where you work and listen to your favorite music while you're at it. You'll find yourself more energized and productive upon returning to your tasks.

You don't have to join a gym to get fit. I'll show you in Chapter 17 some simple and effective exercises you can do in the office or at home. Most smartphones have a built-in app to track your steps. Make it a challenge to walk twenty additional steps each day. After three months, you'll be walking almost 2,000 more steps daily than when you started.

When I make a fitness resolution every year, I examine the trend in my numbers and decide what areas of my body to work on. You see, without monitoring, we have no way of tracking our progress. Instead of debating what we should do, let the numbers point you in the right direction.

Feeling too old to be active? Look at Julia Hawkins. At age 100, she started running. At 103, she won gold medals in both the 50-meter dash and the 100-meter dash at the 2019 Senior Games in Albuquerque, New Mexico.

Stay Hydrated

Drink plenty of water if you don't have any medical conditions that limit your fluid intake. It not only helps skin look healthy but also improves elimination and reduces headaches, pain, dry mouth, and bad breath. The recommended daily intake is eight 8-ounce glasses (think 8 x 8), which equals about two liters or half a gallon. If drinking plain water isn't your thing, try adding flavors to it. Cut up fresh fruits, place them in a water container, and leave it overnight in the refrigerator. The next morning you'll have a refreshing drink to keep you going.

Adopt a Skincare Routine

Hydrate your skin—not just your face, but your whole body. You don't need fancy name products, most of the drug store brands will do. I buy the big jar of Cetaphil moisturizing cream from Costco that lasts for months.

Don't take long, super-hot showers. Hot water strips away the natural oils on your skin, drying it out and reducing its elasticity. After seven years of drought (2011–2017), we Californians have learned to conserve our precious water resource. Play a four-minute song while you shower and see if you can finish before the song ends.

Towel dry and apply a body cream, lotion, butter, or whatever you prefer on still-damp skin (face and neck excluded) to lock in the moisture. Make sure you apply to your back, hands, and feet. Nothing reveals age more than wrinkly necks, hands, and feet. This is one of the easiest slow-aging hacks you will ever use. Notice I didn't say anti-aging. No matter how much money we spend on skin serums, and procedures, we can't stop the effects of time on our bodies. What we can do instead is to slow down the process, making it subtle and less noticeable.

After applying body lotion, use cold water from the faucet to splash your face and neck. While warm water relaxes your skin, a cold rinse causes it to contract immediately. Have you heard of the Finnish bath? That's a hot sauna followed by an ice-cold bath, and it's a proven method to tighten the skin. Cold water promotes blood circulation, which enhances the brightness of your face and makes you look younger.

After towel drying, apply face cream or lotion to your face and neck. I don't recommend using body lotion on your face because facial skin is much thinner than the rest of the body. If you apply heavier product to your face, the excess lotion might accumulate under the skin surface and form small white bumps, especially around the eyes, nose, cheeks, and chin. These are called *milia*, which require a dermatologist to remove them by lancing the bumps one by one to release the trapped content.

After skin hydration, apply sunscreen to your face and neck. Compared to the greasy sunscreen kids smear all over their faces in the summer, there are brands that are lighter in texture and become unnoticeable upon application. Learn to hydrate your skin and apply sunscreen every day—even when it's raining or cloudy. Even in the bad weather, there's enough UV light to damage your skin. If you wear foundation, sunscreen will make it last longer. Try it for yourself.

Be Grateful

There is always someone better than you no matter where you look. You'll drive yourself mad competing with them. If you can't create beautiful things, learn to appreciate them. Instead of using others as markers for your success, think about what brings you the most joy, and do it more often. Learn to let go of bad thoughts so your heart can take in more happiness. Stop living inside your head. Pay attention to the people around you—your partner, your kids, your parents, siblings, and friends. Learn to appreciate their imperfections. Find good intentions from adverse outcomes. Remember, we always find what we're looking for.

13

Four Commandments of Beauty

NO ONE WAKES up beautiful. Don't believe those YouTube videos that showed you otherwise. Some women spend thirty minutes to an hour getting their faces and hair ready before facing the world. Some even go to the extreme of putting on their makeup in crowded commuter trains, detailing their beauty routine in the public eye. Although I encourage women to look good and feel better, I don't agree with the open exhibition of this rather intimate part of our lives. A light touch-up is okay as long as the process is swift. According to *Metro*, the highest-circulation newspaper in the UK, people are bothered by women putting on makeup on public transport.[22] The article explains that the practice breaks down the illusion of women waking up like that, revealing the work that actually goes into a perfectly made-up face. There is also the issue of infringement of personal space. Those women keep elbowing others, their powder and bronzer going everywhere; someone even once dropped her mascara on her seatmate. So if you're short on time in the morning, either wake up earlier to allow enough time for your beauty routine before heading out or simplify your regimen and aim for a subtle and flattering effect.

Some women would call themselves ready when they look like they have just rolled out of bed. They have no time to waste on superfluous things, and they don't care how people view them. I don't agree with this approach either. As I mentioned in Chapter 3, self-appreciation is essential for our happiness. When you let go of your appearance, the mirror of your self-image cracks. You can ignore the crack, but you can't neglect the effect it has on your confidence.

You feel best when you look your best.

The Four Commandments of Beauty

Contrary to common beliefs, beauty isn't absolute—there's no truth in the saying, "Either you're born beautiful or you're not." Beauty is the optimal representation of your inner strengths through your outer appearance. Have you ever seen those remarkable news photos, where the faces of ordinary people look stunning despite the plainness of their features? Being beautiful is letting your inner strengths shine through.

The First Commandment—Face

When it comes to makeup, less is more. Aim to look natural and fresh, not flawless. Your imperfections make you who you are. Don't cover them up just to look the same as everyone else. Enhance your natural strengths so your imperfections become your personal charm, the perfectly imperfect you.

If you aren't comfortable with makeup, here is the world's simplest makeup routine. All you need is a tinted lip balm and ten seconds of time. After completing the skin hydration routine I mentioned earlier, apply tinted lip balm as you would with a lipstick. You'll notice the soft compliment of color on your lips compared to the bold statement of a lipstick. Now sweep the lip balm along your cheekbones and spread the color with your fingers. Yes, you guessed it right, a lip balm can double as a blush to make you look less tired and more polished. Don't fret about the exact location to draw these lines. As you extend the color on your cheeks, you'll see the result of a subtle glow on your skin. If you are in the mood, dab lip balm on your upper eyelids as shadows to enhance the windows to your soul. A lip balm hydrates your skin through nourishing ingredients such as jojoba oil, shea butter, and vitamin E. You can find inexpensive drugstore brands and have a collection of different colors to match your mood and outfit. There are also expensive lines that come with amazing fragrance and packages. I carry mini-sized Fresh Sugar tinted lip treatment in my bag for easy application during the day.

If you want natural rejuvenation, why not try face yoga? It's the facial workout to rewind your biological clock.

Some of you might wonder if face yoga really works. Dr. Murad Alam, the vice chairman of dermatology at Northwestern University, conducted the first clinical trial to assess facial exercise as a modality for improving skin appearance. His team recruited a group of twenty-seven women between the ages of forty and sixty-five to perform facial exercises. At the end of the twenty-week study, the women looked on average three years younger than when they started.[23]

I interviewed Gary Sikorski, the instructor for the study participants.[24] He developed Happy Face Yoga, one of the longest-established facial exercise programs to widen the eyes, lift cheeks, and firm the jawline. Mr. Sikorski designed thirty-two exercises to strengthen and tone all fifty-seven muscles in the face, neck, and scalp. These exercises increase blood circulation, which in turn promotes the production of the natural collagen and elastin in the skin, creating a more vibrant complexion and smoothing fine lines. Regarding the best approach to face yoga, he recommended starting as soon as you see the signs of aging. His advice:

> Pick the exercises focused on your problem areas and practice daily for fifteen to twenty minutes. You can break it up into shorter sessions for convenience. Usually, it takes about two to three weeks to notice softer and more vibrant skin, and four to six weeks for others to notice your youthful look. After ten weeks, you can move on to every other day practice for maintenance."

You can put your facial muscles to work while stuck in traffic, washing your hands in the restroom, or riding in the elevator when no one is around.

The Second Commandment—Hair

Hair plays an essential role in our appearances. As we age, our hair loses its volume and color and becomes frizzy. Our frequent use of chemical treatments, styling irons, and hair dryers lead to more hair damage. A good hair care routine can revitalize your prized locks, restoring the bouncy texture and shine of your natural hair. Use a hydrating hair mask or conditioning treatment at least once a week. If your hair is dry and brittle, consider increasing it to twice weekly. If you don't want to spend money on the name-brand hair treatment, you can make an inexpensive and effective alternative.

Use plain, full-fat mayonnaise from the grocery store for hair conditioning. The fat and oil from mayonnaise can make your hair soft and silky. Use an all-natural, organic product if you can find it. Measure out about a half cup of mayonnaise and let it warm to room temperature before applying to wet hair. Don't use shampoo or conditioner before application. Gently knead your scalp while applying, which helps relieve stress and increase blood circulation to the hair follicles. Use a plastic shower cap to cover your hair for about an hour to allow deep conditioning. If your hair is severely damaged, leave the mayonnaise in overnight. Use shampoo to wash it off. Once your hair returns to normal, use this treatment once a month to keep your hair in a healthy condition.[25]

Get a flattering haircut that suits your personality and lifestyle. This is the only time I encourage you to splurge on a designer cut. It'll take years off your appearance and will make you look confident and sophisticated. If you're happy with the new style but concerned about the maintenance cost, take a picture of your new hairstyle, show it to your regular hairdresser, and ask if he or she can replicate the same cut. If the answer is no, try other salons you can afford until you find the right one.

The Third Commandment—Teeth

Do you know the average American spends 38.5 total days brushing their teeth over a lifetime?[26] Not all of us brush correctly. We should brush using small circular motions, taking care to brush the front, back, and chewing surface of every tooth. This process takes between two and three minutes. Avoid sawing back-and-forth motions. The American Dental Association (ADA) recommends using a toothbrush that has soft bristles.[27] They also advise changing your toothbrush every three months or when the ends look frayed, whichever comes first. Use fluoride-containing toothpaste to prevent cavities. If you don't floss, you miss cleaning 40 percent of your tooth surfaces. Flossing not only reduces dental plaque but also stimulate the gums and helps lower inflammation in the area. Plaque can also build up on your tongue. This leads to bad mouth odor and other oral health problems. Use a tongue scraper, or gently brush your tongue every time you brush teeth. Consider using mouthwash regularly to reduce the amount of acid in the mouth, clean hard-to-brush areas in and around the gums, and re-mineralize the teeth.[28] The late Dr. Perry Ratcliff, one of America's leading periodontists and an expert on dental health and gum disease, created CloSYS, an oral health rinse that's alcohol- and gluten-free and without an overpowering scent. Its patented ingredient Cloralstan® can kill "dental plaque-causing bacteria and volatile sulfur compounds that damage soft tissues."[29]

Some foods and drinks help fight cavities. According to Sheila Brear, a dentistry professor at the University of California, San Francisco, eating hard cheese at the end of a meal helps. Chewing gum for five to ten minutes after a meal can stimulate cavity-thwarting saliva. Drinking tea combats tooth decay as well. Avoid juices and snack foods like chips. When consumed frequently between meals, they can cause tooth decay as much as sugary candies because they're high in carbohydrates, a form of sugar.[30]

Visit your dentist at least twice a year for routine teeth cleanings and checkups. Some of you like your teeth snow-white and use at home or in-office whitening treatment routinely. The two biggest associated concerns are teeth sensitivity and gingival irritation.[31] Consult your dentist before use.

In a multidisciplinary health professional faculty training program a few years ago, my dentist colleague informed me that *linea alba*, the horizontal streak on the inner surface of the cheek, is the indicator of emotional stress. It's much more common among women than men. Think of it as a callus inside the mouth, formed by excess deposits of keratin, a protein found in hair and skin. Stress induces teeth clenching and cheek biting that lead to hyperkeratosis.[32] I spoke to Dr. Mohamed Ali, a former faculty of the Oral and Maxillofacial Surgery department at Loma Linda University, who now maintains a private dental practice in downtown San Francisco. He confirmed the phenomenon. "During my thirty-four years of practice, I've come to know many of my patients well," he said. "When their stress level goes up, I tend to observe more pronounced presentations (of *linea alba*). Although in most cases it's harmless, I like to inform my patients of the stress sign, which often prompts them to make appropriate adjustments to relieve stress."[33]

If your *linea alba* is prominent, consider depressurizing by describing your feelings in a journal (Chapter 6). Try a couple of months of journaling and then recheck your stress line to see if there's any improvement.

The Fourth Commandment—Smile

Kids laugh around 400 times a day; we adults only do so about fifteen times a day. It seems the older we are, the harder it is to enjoy ourselves. Our minds are filled with worries for tomorrow and regrets from yesterday. We're never fully present to enjoy what we do have.

Recently, I went to a conference in Vancouver, BC in Canada, where I met a lady who seemed incapable of smiling. Her face was locked in a scowl as if the world had mistreated her. I tried to make small talk with her, but she wasn't interested in interacting with me. As I write this paragraph, I can see her sitting in the back corner of the room, scanning the crowd as if we had betrayed her. I have no way of knowing if the scowling lady had some traumatic experience that made her that way. Her attitude pushed me away.

A genuine smile is the first thing people notice when they meet you. We're naturally drawn to a warm smile and pleasant demeanor. People with such qualities are usually surrounded by friends and often consider themselves lucky. The longer we stay in negativity, the more miserable we feel and the more unpleasant we appear. If you've been out of practice with smiling for a while, try practicing in the mirror. As Dr. Isha Guptaa, a neurologist from IGEA Brain and Spine, explains, "A smile spurs a chemical reaction in the brain, releasing certain hormones including dopamine and serotonin" that increase our feelings of happiness and reduce stress.

A study performed by a group at the University of Cardiff in Wales found people who could not frown because of Botox injections were happier on average than those who could frown. Researchers at the University of Kansas found that smiling helps reduce the body's response to stress and lowers heart rates during stress recovery. Another study linked smiling to lower blood pressure, while yet another suggested that smiling leads to longevity.[34]

Some women hold the misconception that the more they smile, the more wrinkles they'll have. That is backward thinking. I would choose a cheerful face with lines over a wrinkle-free sour face any day!

14

Dress for Success

IN CHAPTER II we learned to appreciate our bodies, and now is the time to play up our assets and raise our social confidence.

Foundations: Bras and Panties

When it comes to dressing for success, the essential pieces of your wardrobe are the ones people don't see—your bras and panties. Well-fit underwear hugs your body in the right places, making you feel comfortable and at ease. As we age, our bodies change, and so do our breasts, especially after multiple childbirths and breastfeeding. It's important to measure yourself yearly to get the right-sized bras. I keep a record of my measurements on my phone.

According to *Self* magazine, for good bra fit, "you'll need two measurements: around your back and under your bust for your band size, and around your back over your nipples for your cup size. You'll then subtract the difference."[35] If the difference is 1 inch, your cup size is A; 2 inches, size B; 3 inches, size C; and so on.

Years ago, an underwear sales assistant informed me that if I couldn't find my sized bras, I could always go up in the band size and go down in the cup size at the same time or the other way around. For example, both 40B and 36D can fit a 38C. If your annual measurement tends to increase in band size, consider investing in quality bras in your future size when it's on sale. If bra straps are digging into your shoulders, your cups might be too small; if your straps are slipping, then your cups might be too large. For a proper fit, you should be able to pull the bra band on your back without feeling the restriction. Some women like to buy looser bras for more comfort, but those won't give you the lift you need. Look for bras with broad straps to prevent from digging into your skin. You can also try sports bras which provide excellent support and comfort.

For everyday panties, aim for soft, stretchable, and breathable materials that don't rise up. Save those fancy but impractical ones for special occasions where the selected audience would appreciate them. Pretty underwear makes us feel feminine and powerful. If you've been working hard for a while, reward yourself with those cute pieces you can wear every day. It's even better when they're on sale. Sometimes the best emotional support comes from the printed roses resting on your butt cheeks.

Shoes

I could write a whole book about shoes—the funny stories, the traumas, and the frustrations of finding the perfect pair.

My husband and I love traveling overseas. Under his influence, I adopted the concept of travel light with only one piece of carry-on luggage. That means I only wear one pair of shoes on our trips. It takes work to coordinate my outfits with that one pair of shoes so I look decent in our vacation photos. After traveling light for over a decade, I can summarize my conclusions about shoes in three words: first comfort, then quality, and then style.

Think of shoe shopping the way you think about finding a life partner: you want to feel comfortable in them; you want the companionship to last through the seasons; you want them to be reliable and supportive, keeping you moving forward. Would you marry a guy with looks but no substance, who hurt you every step of the way, falling apart at the first sign of a storm? No. You know to invest in someone of quality and character.

Life is hard already, so why put yourself in the wrong shoes and force your feet to fit them? Your body and your thoughts are the only things you have total control over. Relieve yourself from the pain of wearing shoes that aren't a good fit, and spend money on something that will last for years. It's impossible to walk properly in ill-fitting shoes, so step out of them and walk on a new path.

Wardrobe

Take an inventory of your favorite clothes; is there a common color or style that you wear all the time? If the answer is yes, consider experimenting outside of your comfort zone. Thinking those eye-popping colors are too young for you? Well, isn't being youthful what you have been hoping for? Add brightness to your wardrobe and tap into color psychology to boost your energy and happiness. One British study found when evenly matched Olympic athletes competed, those wearing red won significantly more than their blue-wearing opponents.[36] Bright shades draw attention, adding positivity to your persona. Don't go overboard though—you want to be seen as cheerful, but not as a clown, so keep it to one pop color per outfit.

If you struggle to make the leap to color in your basic wardrobes, add colorful accessories: earrings, necklaces, scarves, handbags, shoes, hairbands, or eyeglasses. There are a million ways to entice the audience; you pick the ones that fit you.

There's a growing body of knowledge about how colors affect moods, feelings, and behaviors.[37] I've summarized below some meanings of colors and what they imply in clothing:

COLOR PSYCHOLOGY

Color	Positive Trait	Negative Trait	Clothing Color Meaning
Blue	calmness	sadness	reflective, peaceful
Red	passion	aggressiveness	confident, energetic
Green	safety	envy	compassionate, caring
Yellow	warmth	frustration	cheerful, fresh
Purple	regal	introversion	sensual, mysterious
Brown	reliability	loneliness	reliable, nurturing
Orange	enthusiasm	immaturity	happy, childish
Pink	romance	immaturity	feminine, youthful
Black	power	unhappiness	bold, sophisticated
White	purity	emptiness	clean, innocent

Not everyone responds to colors the same way. Your unique experience could affect how you interpret particular colors.

For example, brown means sickness and bitterness to me. My parents believe in Chinese herbal remedies, and growing up, I drank plenty of those dark brown, bitter liquids—not a happy connotation. Reflect on your memories with different colors. The next time you go shopping, try on the same outfit in various colors to see how you feel in each shade. Dress more in shades that boost your mood and appreciation.

Fashion Rule: Enhance, Don't Cover Up

One common mistake women make is to cover up their bodies, which has the effect of making them look bigger and older than they are. In Chapter 11, you learned to identify your body parts that are in shape. Now it's time to draw attention to your assets through dressing properly. There are a few ways to achieve this effect.

1. **Maximize exposure of your prized body parts.** If you have toned arms, show them off by wearing sleeveless tops in warm weather and a vest over a form-fitting sweater in cold season. If you have nice legs, wear dresses or skirts that show off your shapely assets.
2. **Use bright colors to draw attention to your strong points.** For example, if you have perky breasts, a bright-colored top will bring up the focal point. If you have nice hips, a pair of light-colored pants can highlight your contour well.
3. **Use accessories to enhance your features.** Examples include a colorful or sparkling necklace to accentuate your long neck or a tasteful bangle around your dainty wrist.

Optical Illusions: Trick the Brain to Flatter Your Figure

Based on a study by a Florida State University researcher published in *Clothing and Textiles Research Journal* in 2016, women with a rectangle body shape reacted the most strongly to designs that defined their waists or made them appear curvier. Women with the spoon shape (which carries most of the weight below the waist) were more pleased with the garments that emphasized their bust and shoulders, which balanced out their proportions. The optical illusions used in the study include vertical and horizontal stripes and radial rays.[38]

If you have a tall and boyish frame, consider wearing dresses or tops with darker patches of fabric around the waistline. This creates an hourglass effect, making you appear more feminine. You can also wear a belt to define your waistline, choosing a width that is proportional to your size. These recommendations also work if you tend to carry weight in the midsection.

As to stripes, "diagonal lines are incredibly slimming," and the closer the vertical lines are spaced together, the slimmer you'll look. For horizontal lines, the longer an eye travels up or down a body before it is interrupted by a horizontal line, the taller and leaner you will look … this is also why contrast colored belts are not advisable for petite women. Cutting this body shape in half … makes you look wider … (and) shorter."[39]

For tall women, wearing your top and bottom in different colors will create the vertical divide and soften your height. For women with short legs, wearing a pair of loose-fitting trouser pants or bootcut jeans with a comfortable heel can elongate your legs and make you appear taller.

The length rule: stop where it should. If you want to achieve a slimming effect, the best length for your dress is when the bottom seam stops at the thinner part of your leg, either just below the knees or below your calves where your legs taper down. If you wear capri pants, make sure they are ankle length to create the same flattering result.

Walk Like a Woman

Having you ever seen a military tank moving, its bottom heavy and upper body leaning forward? Unfortunately, that is how a lot of us walk. Not feminine at all.

Keep the center of your upper and lower body in a vertical line, not bent forward or backward. Walk with your shoulders relaxed and level, your eyes looking right in front of you, not down at the pavement like you lost a lottery ticket. Elongate your neck. If you're not blessed with a long neck, this is particularly important. When you walk, you should not be able to see your shoulders unless you turn your head.

Don't swing your arms far away from your body as you walk. You are not racing, so there's no need for the arms to propel you. If you ever watch elderly women walk across the street, they swing their arms a lot faster than they move their legs. It gives off the impression of aging and frailty. Swing your arms naturally and coordinate with your steps.

Practice your new walking style five minutes a day until you don't feel like a robot anymore. Watch your kids move about and try to infuse that youthful energy into your gait.

15

Jazz It up in Bed

LET'S FACE IT: kids are the best birth control ever invented. If you're like most of us, sex is the last thing you want when you get into bed at the end of a long day. Your mind is heavy with worries, and your body aches like you've been fighting all day. When your man's hand finds its way to you under the sheets, your lips move before your brain even processes it: "Please, not tonight."

Does that sound familiar?

The truth is, as a working mom, your days will most likely be busy, and you'll end up feeling tired most nights. If you're waiting for the perfect time to renew your passion, it's like waiting for Halley's Comet to visit every seventy-five years. Few marriages can sustain a long drought without falling apart. Don't think you're in the safe zone just because your partner hasn't complained about it yet. It's usually the things left unsaid that keep couples apart.

Denise Donnelly, professor of sociology at Georgia State University, estimates one in seven married couples did not have sex with their partner in the last six to twelve months.[40] Are you one of them?

Michele Weiner-Davis, author of *The Sex Starved Marriage*, explains why a low-sex marriage is a major problem:

When this major disconnect happens, intimacy at all levels drops. It's about feeling wanted, feeling loved, feeling appreciated, and feeling connected and, in this case, feeling feminine. Because of the hurt, [a couple stops] spending time together. They stop laughing at each other's jokes. They stop making eye contact. The bond between them dissipates, and it puts the marriage at risk for infidelity and divorce.[41]

Health Benefits of Sex

If the only reason you're withholding sex is because of stress, the surprising health benefits of sex might change your mind. Health experts agree that having a healthy, active sex life is good for you. Some health benefits include:

1. **Keeping the immune system strong.** Researchers at Wilkes University in Pennsylvania found that people who had sex once or twice per week had more immunoglobulin A antibody in their system than others.[42] Found in mucous membranes in the respiratory and digestive tracts, Immunoglobulin A helps fight infections such as the common cold and flu.

2. **Providing a good pelvic floor workout.** Pregnancy, childbirth, and other factors weaken the pelvic floor muscles and may lead to incontinence later in life. Good sex may help strengthen the weakened muscles. "Women tell me that after paying more attention

to the control and coordination of their pelvic floor muscles, they have found new heights to their sensation and awareness during sex," Kathryn Warr, Founder of IvoryRose Physiotherapy for Her, told The Huffington Post Australia.[43]

3. **Improving mood, memory, and sleep.** Sex triggers the release of oxytocin, endorphins, and other "feel-good" hormones responsible for the stress-reducing effect.[44] A 2017 study showed the frequency of sex was positively associated with memory function in heterosexual women.[45] Researchers also found people who had orgasms before bed (either from intercourse or masturbation) experienced improved sleep quality.[46] Sex might just be the all-natural sleeping aid you've been looking for.

4. **Blocking pain.** Barry Komisaruk, a distinguished psychology professor at Rutgers University, found that vaginal self-stimulation more than doubled the women's pain thresholds.[47] A 2013 study in Germany showed that sexual activities could relieve or even stop a migraine attack in both men and women. Subjects with cluster headaches also felt better after sex.[48]

5. **Preventing prostate cancer.** According to a study published in the Journal of the American Medical Association, men who ejaculated frequently were less likely to get prostate cancer.[49] If you truly love your man, you would do anything to help him live longer and healthier, wouldn't you?

6. **Rejuvenating your skin.**[50] If you make love regularly, you'll have the happy glow that makes others envy you. Think of your partner as a super Botox/filler machine who can revitalize your appearance for free. Instead of paying a beauty spa every few months, use that money to take your entire family on vacation. When your coworkers inquire what you've done to

look so good, tell them it's a special formula designed just for you.

Keeping a regular sex routine takes planning. Have an honest conversation with your partner and work out a schedule that both parties approve. Stick to the plan no matter how tired you are. You'll feel better afterward. It's much easier to fall asleep after sex, and you'll wake up the next day energized and cheerful.

Not in the Mood?

You may not feel sexy after the children, but there are tools that can put you in the right mood immediately. It only takes five seconds to get that super lacy lingerie out of the drawer, and another ten seconds to put it on and make a grand entrance. When you dress sexy, you feel more confident. When you feel sexy, your body responds sensually, much to your partner's delight. He will be more than willing to please you in bed—and out of bed. If he has been forgetful about the chores you give him, remind him after sex. Trust me, he will remember every word you say, down to the letter. Talk about the power of sex.

Out of Practice?

Don't worry about how out of practice you feel. The more you do it, the better you'll become and the more benefits you'll receive. Regular sex increases the level of trust and intimacy in your relationship. You'll find yourself more open to your man; you'll talk more about how you feel and how you feel about him. He'll appreciate your trust, and in return, he'll care for you more. He will want to offer solutions to your problems. When you appreciate his effort, he feels proud of himself and becomes motivated to do more for you. Even if his recommendation doesn't work, thank him anyway. He cares about you; that's what matters. Most men don't know how to comfort women, in my opinion. Find your best buddies to process your emotions; they'll understand you better.

Spice It Up

To spice up your bedtime activities, setting the right ambiance can help both you and your partner to relax and enjoy. Turn on the romantic playlist; light a scented candle if you desire. Have your partner massage you if you're tense. Caress him if he is not ready. Use lubricant or stimulating gel to enhance your pleasure. During sex, say what you want him to do, and watch him try his best to please you. Tell him what he makes you feel to validate his effort. If you need help to reach orgasm, try using a vibrator to intensify the experience. Everyone has sexual fantasies. Knowing your partner's will help turn him into a sex machine made just for you. It's nothing short of a wonder that out of seven billion people on earth, you married each other and had children together. Fuel your loving relationship with sexual intimacy. When your children grow up in a household filled with love, they'll be more likely to have happy marriages of their own.

Remember, what happens between you and him in bed is nobody else's business. Be wild, be silly, be quirky—whatever works to keep your passion going strong for the years to come.

When Passion Is Missing

Some of you may no longer be attracted to your partner, or perhaps never were. Unhappy about the situation, you're probably used to the emotional distance between you and your partner. If you intend to stay married, instead of longing for what is missing, try to focus on the positive aspects of your relationship. Do something fun and exciting with your partner to warm up to each other. During intimacy, focus on how you feel rather than how disappointing your partner is. The shift in perspective can boost your level of satisfaction. Even though you may never fall in love with your partner, you'll learn to appreciate his loyalty and to see more of his virtues than shortcomings.

If you love your partner but he's no longer intimate with you, try to uncover the real cause. Has he been stressed about work, or do certain medications affect his libido? If the cause is related to stress, help him resolve the issue by figuring out a solution together. If it's related to medical causes, talk to his doctor as a couple to seek treatment or switch to alternatives.

Stop thinking about how awkward you look and immerse yourself in action. Imagine yourself being twenty-one again, tease him until he responds, then resist him until he's fully engaged. Do what your twenty-one-year-old body would do and think what your younger mind would believe. He'll feel the difference in you and respond to your newfound passion. Lovemaking is an art—it's not the body that matters, it's the mind that makes the magic happen.

To All the Single Ladies

Last, if you're single, invest in a good vibrator that can liberate you from all inhibitions. You'll experience all the benefits mentioned above. Schedule time for your solo session where you can rewind and revitalize. You'll feel like a brand-new person.

Here's to all you undercover sexy ladies!

16

The Food Truth

WEIGHT GAIN IS women's number one concern about their bodies. With each passing year, our metabolisms slow down more. It seems entirely possible that we get rounder just by drinking water. Everyone knows to eat in moderation, but when the serving plates and drink sizes keep getting bigger and bigger, our brains are tricked into believing we aren't eating that much. Even clothing brands have accommodated our ever-growing bodies by shrinking the numbers in sizes to make us feel good. According to *The Washington Post*, "A size 8 dress today is nearly the equivalent of a size 16 dress in 1958."[51]

From the South Beach Diet to Paleo to Keto, so many popular diets promise weight loss by asking us to deny ourselves. Sooner or later, cravings for the foods we deny ourselves will exhaust our willpower, and we'll go back to the old routines. Instead of aiming for weight loss alone, think about your overall wellness—a sense of happiness and fulfillment, flexibility, endurance, organ function, and bone health.

Is there a way to improve our mental and physical health by eating? Nutritional science researchers from the University of California, San Francisco (UCSF) and University of California, San Diego (UCSD)[52] recommend the following.

Take Every Piece of Nutrition Advice with a Grain of Salt

"Nutrition research is an imperfect and evolving field," the article's authors write. "Take the '80s advice to follow a low-fat diet. It triggered a billion-dollar industry of low-fat, high-sugar food with little nutritional value … and contributed to a public health crisis marked by skyrocketing rates of diabetes." Dr. Frederick Hecht, the Osher Foundation professor and director of research at the UCSF Osher Center for Integrative Medicine, offers, "We, as a field, have made huge mistakes. We need to better convey the limitations of current science when providing advice."

Beware of Healthy-Sounding Products and Supplements

If you can, skip the packaged foods altogether and eat only things your grandmother would recognize. "Unless you know you have a specific nutritional deficiency, supplements could do more harm than good. We just don't know," the article's authors suggest. "Unlike prescription medications, the FDA has few regulations for supplement manufacturers. In fact, supplements are considered safe by the FDA until proven otherwise."

Treat Food as Medicine

UCSF family physician Daphne Miller, MD, "spent years traveling and researching the healthiest regions around the globe. She wrote her first book, *The Jungle Effect*, on the traditional diets and recipes that had kept those communities healthy for generations. In the process, she came to see the dramatic link between certain diets and a striking lack of chronic diseases, including heart disease, depression, diabetes, colon cancer, breast cancer, and prostate cancer."

Try incorporating these healthy habits into your diet:

- Eat five to nine servings of produce per day, and eat more vegetables than fruits.
- Buy organic produce whenever possible.
- Eat cruciferous vegetables (broccoli, cauliflower, brussels sprouts, kale) every day.
- Don't overcook vegetables—steam, blanch, or stir-fry them.
- Buy organic chicken, and go easy on the eggs.
- Eat unprocessed soy (tofu, soybeans, soy milk) and avoid processed soy like fake cheese or meats.
- Limit meat consumption.
- Avoid processed meats and refined sugar.
- Incorporate turmeric into your diet as an anti-inflammatory.

Restrict When You Eat

"Try eating [three meals] within an eight- to 10-hour window can help fend off disease and have more energy," says Dr. Satchin Panda, a worldwide expert on circadian rhythms research. "Almost every organ in our body has an internal clock that tells our systems when to wake, sleep, eat, and perform other functions. A growing body of research suggests that for optimal health, we need to abide by these innate rhythms. ... Just as the brain needs sleep, our digestive organs need downtime to repair and rejuvenate." Your stomach, liver, intestines, and other organs need to cleanse, which takes between twelve and fourteen hours. By sticking to a consistent eating window every day, your body will know when to expect food.

Introduce Kids to Healthy Eating

Katie Ferraro, MPH, an associate clinical professor of nutrition at UCSF, offers the following advice:

> Some flavor compounds are transmitted through breast milk. If a mother mixes up her diet while breastfeeding, the baby's future palate may benefit. Data show picky eaters tend to come from households where parents have limited variety in their diet. Broadening your food horizons will encourage your kids to do the same. Research shows the more textures and flavors kids are exposed to early in life, the greater food acceptance they'll display down the road. Some babies need to try a new food about 10 to 15 times before they'll like or accept it. Try offering the same foods prepared in different ways—boiled, roasted, baked, broiled. Cook with your kids. Start as young as you can. Have them mix, chop, sprinkle, stir. If they help prepare a meal, they will be more inclined to eat it."

The Bottom Line

Stop chasing diet fads. Treat foods as medicine—watch what you eat and when you eat. Eat real food—not supplements—to recharge. Fuel your body with nature's best ingredients for optimal health.

17

The Super Workout

MANY WORKING MOMS want to exercise for weight loss; few achieve their goals. I've heard all kinds of reasons for their inaction—from too busy to a tight budget to lack of willpower or workout buddy. The underlying message is *I'll get it done once I have everything I need.*

What if you never get what you need?

The truth is, life is never perfect. As soon as we fix a problem, another one pops up. It's the ongoing challenge that makes us stronger and wiser than before.

Remember, it's not the strongest of the species that survives, nor the most intelligent that survives. It is the one that is the most adaptable to change.

Being adaptive means we take action using the limited resources we have. Instead of waiting for the elusive perfect future, think about how you can make things happen despite the challenges. There are ways to overcome the obstacles regardless of how difficult your situation may seem. Later in this chapter, I'll show you how to tackle specific concerns.

Some of you might shake your heads, thinking, *Well, I tried working out before, but it didn't help me lose weight. So I quit.* I hear you. Practicing something while getting no rewards can be demoralizing. When that happens, ask yourself these questions:

Did I have the right goal?
Did I have the right approach to reach my goal?
Did I maximize my chance of success?

Set the Right Goal

To achieve your desired outcome, you need to set the right goal. Instead of being motivated by health concerns, most women focus on weight loss only. They believe being thinner will make them happier and more attractive. While losing weight may improve your blood pressure and blood sugar, it isn't the key to happiness. I have met many unhappy thin women in my life; so have you. Attractiveness is the product of inner health (both mental and physical), outer appearance, and social confidence. You need the whole package to boost your attractiveness.

Set the goal to achieve your optimal health, not weight loss alone. The former is a state of mind, the latter a numbers game. Pay attention to how your mind and body work together. You are likely in tune with the internal feedback and adjust your habits naturally. In Chapter 6, I recommended the practice of journaling about your emotions. The same method applies to your diet. Record what you eat, when you eat, and how various foods make you feel. This way, you'll discover why you crave certain junk foods, and then you can experiment with healthy alternatives to achieve the same emotional comfort.

Identify Your Approach

Next, you need to understand your body type. Different body types need different workout approaches to achieve optimal results.[53] For those who have given up on fitness, pay special attention here.

Ectomorphs have the marathon runner type of body. Their long and lean form and fast metabolism make it difficult for them to build muscle and fat. To bulk up, they need to consume a diet high in complex carbohydrates and protein and practice compound movements that involve multiple big muscle groups, such as squats, lunges, and jumping ropes.

Endomorphs have the round body shape, storing most of their muscle and fat in their lower body. They have a slow metabolism, so it's easier to pack on weight. Reducing carbohydrates intake while increasing protein and fiber consumption may help them slim down. High-intensity interval training (HIIT) can speed up their metabolism and promote fat burning for hours after they work out. This type of exercise burns calories by giving maximal effort in short, intense bursts.

Mesomorphs are the athletic type who is both lean and muscular. Because of their fast metabolism and ability to build and maintain muscles, a diet comprising 40 percent complex carbohydrates, 30 percent lean protein, and 30 percent healthy fats is the most beneficial. Similar to endomorphs, their staple workout is HIIT.

Maximize Your Chance of Success

After setting the right goal and identifying your approach, you need to maximize your chance of success by eliminating the negative factors that could sabotage your effort. Bad habits are much easier to pick up than good ones. That is because bad habits are easily obtainable and convenient with instant gratification. Good habits take willpower, and rewards are often delayed. People quit doing the right thing because of the constant temptation of bad habits and a lack of self-control.

Why don't you turn workouts into fun activities with your family? No one says you have to exercise alone. With children spending more and more time on digital devices, the traditional sense of playing outdoors has become an unfamiliar concept. Reintroduce the idea by bringing them to a park or playing in your backyard, where you can hear the birds chirping and feel the breeze. Research in a growing scientific field called *ecotherapy* has shown a strong connection between time spent in nature and reduced stress, anxiety, and depression. Even listening to recorded nature sounds can have a similar effect. Researchers have found supporting evidence in brain activities shown on MRI.[54]

If your kids are old enough to take part in the actual workout, have them join you and make it a game. For example, the person who can jump rope the longest is the champion. Older children might even give feedback on your form. If they are too young to join you, assign them to be your timekeeper and cheerleader. Children mightn't be the best listeners, but they're great imitators. Seeing you active may influence your kids to continue a healthy lifestyle when they grow up.

Have a backup plan if bad weather or other things prevent you from working out outdoors. HIIT requires no equipment except a timer. Each move takes less than a minute, followed by a short rest. You can finish the entire workout in under thirty minutes and still burn the same amount of calories as if you went jogging for an hour. The best part is you only need to do HIIT two or three times a week, and then you simply walk the other days. Combine this with a healthy diet you'll see results in just a few weeks.

Scheduling Is Key

Set aside protected workout time. Make it a part of your daily routine. Based on a study published in the *European Journal of Social Psychology*, it takes on average sixty-six days before a new behavior becomes automatic.[55] If sixty-six days seem too long for you, learn from comedian Jerry Seinfeld's productivity tip—"Don't Break the Chain." Every day Seinfeld wrote a joke, he marked a big X on a wall calendar. Once he had a nice, long X chain on the calendar, all he wanted to do was not to break that chain.[56] Apply this technique to any challenge; the idea is to take it one day at a time. Stop thinking about how many more days you have to do something and focus instead on just getting the day's task done.

Start small and practice often. This way, you can overcome the fear of failure and are likely to experience the joy of getting more done with each passing day. If physical limitations and health conditions prevent you from being fully functional, check with your doctor first before attempting any strenuous activities.

High-Intensity Interval Training

Japanese scientist Izumi Tabata first studied the HIIT method in 1996. Compared to moderate-intensity continuous training for 60 minutes, a 4-minute HIIT workout led to higher muscle power output and aerobic endurance after 6 weeks. [57] A wide variety of HIIT programs have since been developed to promote cardio fitness and body composition. You can check out the example workout routine published in *Self* magazine. [58]

Overcome Excuses

Let's revisit the concerns you may have toward starting or maintaining a regular exercise schedule.

- Lack of results: Not all workouts are created equal, so explore new exercises that can get you in shape sooner. Try new workouts using the introductory discount at e-commerce sites like Groupon or LivingSocial. Those sites run deeply discounted deals for trial membership or class cards. That was how I found my yoga studio ten years ago. Or visit a local gym and get a complimentary trial pass to see if it fits your personality and lifestyle.

- Too busy and no budget: Use the low-price trial offer to get yourself familiarized with a workout routine, then practice at home with your kids.

- Lack of patience: Instead of weighing yourself every day, record how you feel post-workout. After a few weeks of journaling, you'll likely see an improvement in your mood, energy, and focus. Soon you'll find one workout more enjoyable than others. Stick to the exercise that makes you feel better, and your body will transform over time. You'll also be more motivated to eat healthily as you become more active.

- No workout buddy: Exercise with your children. Assign them the role of your accountability partner and enjoy your quality time together.

- Lack of willpower: Use a wall calendar, and never break the chain.
- Boring workout: Switch up your routine and your playlist.

Have You Heard? Sitting Is the New Smoking

According to the Internal Osteoarthritis Foundation, seven out of ten women over the age of thirty-five suffer joint pains.[59] One of the most common reasons is obesity; the other is we don't stretch enough. From home to work, we sit far too long, and our range of motions become smaller than ever. Remember the scene in the animated film *WALL_E*, where humans have stubby limbs and round middles that make us look more like walking eggs? If we don't get up and move more, that funny scene may not be a distant future.

Do you feel discomfort when you bend down to pick up the pen you dropped? When our bodies are not in perfect alignment, we experience stiffness and pain. Yoga can improve your flexibility and posture. If you don't have time or budget for a yoga studio membership, try participating in a work-trade program where you help out at a yoga studio in exchange for unlimited classes. If that doesn't work, use a free yoga app to get yourself familiar with the poses. Healthline. com recommends Daily Yoga as the best yoga app of 2019.[60]

I have been practicing Bikram yoga (hot yoga) for a decade. It helps me with sleep, anxiety, and patience. I enjoy taking a shower after a sweaty ninety-minute session and feel cleansed inside and out. My skin glows after the workout. If you can't stand the heat, regular yoga works as well. Researchers found no difference in cardiovascular health between room temperature yoga and hot yoga.[61]

Michele Vennard, winner of the Adult 50+ Women's Division Gold Medal at the 2018 USA Yoga Nationals and the Silver Medal in the 2017 Nationals, has been teaching yoga for over twenty years, mostly out of her elegant studio in Silicon Valley. She was a marketing director for a successful Italian restaurant group prior to her yoga career. Watch the video recording of her 2018 competition.[62] At age fifty-four, her body extruded energy and grace.

"Different from other types of exercise," she told me, "Bikram yoga is a total body workout designed to improve blood circulation, spinal traction and articulation, respiratory, digestive, and endocrine function, lymphatic drainage, and fascia (connective tissue) release among other things. These 'invisible' changes rejuvenate our bodies in the aging process.

"Besides the physical benefits, it's also an open-eye meditation that gives you a sense of calmness, clarity, and confidence. It helped me cope with my mother's death. That was when I realized I want to teach and spread this message from our founder, Bikram Choudhury, 'Never too old, never too sick, never too late to do yoga and start from scratch … again.'"

Michele's studio offers onsite childcare. She recommends busy moms take advantage of such services in their local communities and enjoy yoga as a mental and physical "retreat." Moms can also look for places that offer early or late classes so they can practice either before kids wake up or after they are in bed.[63]

Set the right goal, identify your approach, and incorporate exercise into your daily routine. Be the champion in your household to get active and positive. Your health will improve, and so will your figure.

THE PATH

Your path is your journey
From confusion to confidence to courage,
From trying to fit in to designing the life you deserve
May grit be your fuel, strengths your direction, and loved ones the tailwind.
Sail on, mothers, sisters, and daughters, be the heroine in your own life.
Brave the weathers, and crush the waves,
You're perfect in your own imperfect ways.
To your true north!

18

The Impossible Dream

DID YOU HAVE a dream that used to keep you up at night as you wondered about all of its possibilities? Do you still think about it when you're frustrated and wish you had taken your chance when you were younger and bolder? It's too late now, you may say.

Is it?

I wanted to be an actress when I was little.

I begged my parents to let me go to the movies, and I watched those movies with feverish imagination. I edited the scenes in my head and wrote in my diaries how I could improve the delivery. Needless to say, I wasn't any good, but the drive to create great stories motivated me to read and write. My dream was to be the actress who could write her own script and bring the audience into a world she made real.

I loved to sing and dance and started performing on stage at age three. I would impersonate celebrities with my childish charm. My mom told me that my poetry recitals made the grown-ups laugh and cry. At school, I was in all the campus musical performances. In high school, I had to decide about pursuing a career. That was when I learned there was a profession called the starving artist.

Ever since I could remember, my parents reminded me, "Don't do this, it's not good; don't do that, it's bad for you." Growing up, I had this constant fear of messing up my life if I didn't listen.

They told me I needed a "real" job, the kind that provided a stable income and respectable social status. So I studied business in college, which landed me the job working for the airline executives. I soon learned the corporate world wasn't for me. I yearned for creativity and innovation. After receiving a master's degree in engineering, I transferred to the technical side of the same airline. That wasn't for me either.

Soon I left the airline and moved to San Francisco to marry my husband. For two months I stayed at home, debating what to do next. Once again, my childhood aspiration made its way back to my dreams. I thought about the theater performances I had given in college—how ecstatic I was to see the audience applaud for the Jane Eyre I played on stage. Then the reality sank in—if I couldn't be a starving artist when I was single, how could I do that when attached?

Every day I sat at a desk, filling the columns of the pros and cons of various career options. It didn't help. Both of my previous jobs had more pros than cons, but I wasn't happy. I felt trapped by the corporate rules. Besides what my parents told me, I felt strongly that a real job should have a third component, a deep sense of fulfillment. If I couldn't be an actress who changes lives through her artistic performances, I wanted to help people in a field that allowed me the freedom to use my talent and expertise. I became a pharmacist.

In the winter of 2016, Warner Brothers' feature film *Crazy Rich Asians* had an open casting call for several of its major roles. The news invigorated my dormant dream. I got professional portraits done and wrote my resume. It was then I realized how long it had been since my last performance. I scrutinized my face in the mirror. There had to be scores of younger and prettier women with regular screen time who would outcompete me. In the end, I put away the portraits and saved the resume on my laptop. A year later, when the movie was in production, I read that the film's many supporting actors had little or no acting background. I wished I had submitted the application. Even though the result might have been the same, I had owed it to myself to give it a shot.

With each passing year, being a successful actress has felt more like an impossible dream. But I have found an equally exciting alternative to fuel my creative passion—being a writer. I finished a political thriller this year. A Hollywood producer liked the novel so much that he wants to represent me and bring the story to the screen. This book is my second project. By the time you read this passage, I should be well into my third book, a psychological thriller.

Life is never meant to go as planned, at least not for me. Each mistake I make teaches me something about myself, who I am, and where I want to be. Though I'm not an expert in career planning, I encourage you to dig deep into your old dream and find out why it was so important to you. In Chapter 2, you learned how to identify your strengths. Now, record in your journal the struggles you have in searching for your true north. Let the words bring clarity to your thoughts.

Connect the dots between your aspiration and your natural talent, and then pick the shortest route to proceed.

Finding purpose in life is like spotting the lighthouse beacon in the dark, vast ocean. It keeps you from living blind-folded in the mind-numbing routine. With courage and careful planning, you'll set sail on the path to fulfillment in due course.

19

Reverse Engineer
Your Path

BEFORE YOU DECIDE where you want to be, you must first examine where you came from.

Think about how the events of the past led you to the present and in what way they have shaped your life. What is missing from your life now? What change do you yearn for when staring into the darkness on those sleepless nights?

In the last chapter, I talked about the importance of our old dreams, the wholehearted devotion we had in our younger years. That was our joy in its purest form, untouched by money, status, and responsibilities. Few had the courage and stamina to push through resistance to pursue that dream. Even fewer reached their goals. Most of us let circumstances dictate our courses of action. Before we knew it, we had drifted away from the path meaningful to us.

Some dreams are hard to carry out at a later time, like my acting career or your gymnastic talent. What matters are the reasons behind our passions. Why were those dreams so important to us? What did we experience when we practiced so hard to explore our potentials?

My desire for being a successful actress was rooted in the creative drive to bring great stories to life. Acting was the most visual and persuasive method to make that happen. Once I figured out that creativity was my passion, I started writing right away. Though I may never be a great writer, I aim to put out my best work. Writing this book forces me to look deeper inside myself, pick apart my scars, analyze my mistakes and detours, and present you the authentic depiction of a working mom's journey to be happier, healthier, and get more out of life. I become a better human being through writing. It brings focus to my chaotic days and anchors me to the essentials in life—love, joy, and appreciation.

By examining your past, you will likely see a pattern or a sign of your previous struggles that will guide you to get back on the path meant for you. Take out your notebook and write an entry whenever some random event brings back the forgotten memory. Jot down how it makes you feel now as compared to then. Distill your thoughts and emotions through writing. This is the process of knowing yourself as the person who you were born to be, rather than who you think you are.

Don't rush the process. Everyone is different. A complicated life takes longer to process. Be patient and truthful with your words. It takes time to recognize your calling. If you keep trying, it'll become clear to you.

Once you have a clear vision of where you want to be, you'll want to take actions right away. But hang on, two things are critical at this stage: courage and careful planning. Miss either of the two and you won't succeed. Courage will enable you to push through resistance, both internal and external, especially from your loved ones. You'll need the courage to keep going when things are not going well despite your efforts. Careful planning will save you time, resources, and unnecessary frustrations. It's a growth map that keeps you focused on the end goal.

In this chapter, I'll show you how to plan your course of action by reverse engineering. Simply put, you need to analyze the people who have achieved what you are looking for and identify the steps leading to their success. Go to LinkedIn or Facebook and find these influencers and take notes on their employment history or career path. What credentials do they have, and what organizations do they belong to? Join the organizations and explore the opportunities to connect with them. Be helpful to them so they'll be willing to support you in return. Build a mutually beneficial relationship and find the right person to be your mentor. Because everyone is different, you must tease out the individual variations and focus on the commonalities among these experts. Once you confirm all the necessary steps, examine how long each step takes and the easiest way to complete it, and come up with your personal road map.

For example, if you want to start a small business by selling your artistic creations online, the first thing to do is to look for people who are already successful in the field. Study their websites to learn about their products, pricing, and distribution channels. Go to local trade association events and speak to people who have already been doing what you're hoping to start. Ask them about their journeys to success, and what words of wisdom they can share with you. Offer samples of your products for sale on their platforms to test the market. To maximize the chance of collaboration, tell them they can keep all the profits from your samples. If your products sell well, propose a mutually beneficial profit split so you can make money by using their established clientele. If yours didn't do well, ask for their feedback, and follow up with a revised design. You can collaborate with multiple experts while building a following for your own brand. When the time comes, you can begin your solo venture. By then, people will want to ask *you* for words of advice. Be generous in helping others. Life is never a zero-sum game. The more helpful you are, the more talented people you'll attract, and the better opportunities you'll get through collaboration.

When I decided to be a writer, I began immediately working on a story I had been thinking about for a while. When the novel was completed four months later, it was terrible. The plot wasn't cohesive, and the characters were wimpy. My first reaction was that I lacked talent. I thought I needed to join a reputable, low-residency master of fine arts (MFA) program and learn to be a writer. These two-year-long programs are costly. All require a few weeks of onsite training each year, which would inevitably cut my family vacation time. Counting the postdoctoral training, I had spent a significant part of my life in school. Getting another degree wasn't something I was eager to pursue.

I started writing a second novel while debating if an MFA was necessary for me. Although I'm a pantser (someone who writes without an outline), I outlined the story I wanted to tell. By identifying the plot points in a three-act structure, I stopped drifting off course. I began borrowing books on writing from the library and read them whenever I needed inspiration or encouragement. I went to various writers conferences and met other like-minded souls. I joined local literary events to become comfortable telling others I was a writer. With the second novel, my writing flowed better. The characters seemed to have gained some muscles and begun to stand on their own. I no longer felt embarrassed reading my own creation. After I completed the draft, I was convinced that I didn't need another degree. I can improve my writing by practicing and learning from the masters. That was how I started my third novel, the political thriller mentioned earlier.

How to Excel in Any Field

If you truly want to excel in your field, the following growth mindsets are essential.

1. **Keep your motives pure, and it'll show in your work.** You are pursuing your dream for the very reason it's important to you. Not for money or status. For example, if I set out to get rich and famous by writing, I would second-guess myself on every page, trying to predict what readers want to see and how the market would trend. The quality of my writing would suffer, and my work would never exceed the commercial value it's attached to. I want to be a writer, not a peddler.

2. **Practice patience.** Everything worthwhile takes time. There's no miracle growth in excellence. Take each failure as an opportunity to improve. Challenge your mind to see things differently; take things apart and rearrange them in brand-new ways to give your work new meaning. The road to success is paved with the constant struggle to reach beyond limitations.

3. **Celebrate your wins, big and small.** Every step you take on this journey is a breakthrough from your old self. Record your accomplishments along the way.

These mini milestones serve as a reminder of how much you've grown since you started. Be proud of your progress. You're on a path that few dare to take. Not everyone can be the master of their time, but you can strive to be the master of your own life.

20

Time Management

IN 2014, I went to Philadelphia to present my research findings at the Infectious Diseases Society of America Annual
Meeting. I remember sitting in the audience listening to a
speaker talking about modern diseases. As I write this passage, his words echo in my ears: most of our ailments are
manmade, caused by *curry, hurry, and worry.*

We touched on *hurry* in Chapter 5, "Live Simply," where
we discuss how to slow down and appreciate what is meaningful to us. In his presentation, the speaker explained that
curry is a representation of too much indulgence in food that
doesn't serve us. We addressed the issue in Chapter 17, "The
Food Truth." Now let's take a look at excessive worry.

Worry

How often we neglect to care for our bodies until they fall apart. Whenever I talk to working moms about self-care, the first thing they say is usually, *But I just don't have time for it.* When I ask if they worry a lot, they tell me they worry all the time.

Does it make sense that we spend all of our time worrying but no time taking action? Worrying doesn't protect us from disasters and disappointments. It clouds our mind, making it difficult to see the steps we should take. As a result, we let problems dictate our actions.

Have you noticed that you can hardly recall what happened yesterday? Everything blurs into an undifferentiated mass with no clear separation of yesterday, today, and tomorrow. Everything becomes automatic without a higher level of engagement. I call this *zombie living.* We must learn to be engaged in our daily lives so we don't miss the important things. Trimming down the extra weight we carry, in mind and body, will help us live a productive life.

How to better use time? Some techniques you can try are eliminating distractions and focusing on what's important, multitasking the smart way, and optimizing your time.

Eliminate, then Prioritize

As crucial as it is to figure out what to do, you also need to decide what not to do. Because we have limited time and energy, we want to eliminate distractions and focus on essential things. First, automate time-consuming routine tasks such as buying household supplies by setting up monthly deliveries online. Next, delegate age-appropriate chores to each of your kids and set up a weekly competition to reward your best-performing "employee." They'll gain essential life skills, and you'll have time for the important stuff.

Sometimes we have trouble deciding what is important to us. Remember, time is money. Think about your end goal when examining the list of responsibilities. What are the action steps that can get you closer to that goal? If something serves your purpose, keep it; if not, eliminate it.

After the elimination round, it's time to prioritize tasks to maximize the gain on your time investment. This is a two-step process.

First, evaluate the urgency of each task. Rank them from the most urgent to the least. You should always do the most pressing one first.

Second, prioritize the less-urgent tasks by estimating the ratio of reward/time requirement. The higher the ratio, the higher the task ranks.

For example, on my day off, I have the following tasks to do:

- ☐ Research a summer internship opportunity for Ethan
- ☐ Proofread the chapter I wrote the night before
- ☐ Buy milk and eggs
- ☐ Label the holiday greeting cards and mail them out
- ☐ Pick up Chu from the airport at 10:15 a.m.

So my ranking process will look like this:

Based on the urgency level, picking up my husband should rank first on my list. Researching for an internship opportunity has high reward but will probably take hours, so the reward/time requirement ratio is average. Proofreading my book chapter only takes fifteen minutes and will award me with great satisfaction, so the reward/time requirement ratio is high. Buying groceries and labeling and mailing cards take about the same amount of time and give me the same level of satisfaction. But buying milk is more urgent because if I don't get it done, Ethan won't have any milk that night. I can mail the cards any day before Christmas, thus not as urgent. Because the post office is on my way to the store, I can drop off the cards before buying milk.

Here's my final ranking of tasks:

1. *Pick up Chu from the airport at 10:15 a.m.*
2. *Proofread the chapter I wrote the night before*
3. *Label the holiday greeting cards and mail them out, then buy milk and eggs*
4. *Research a summer internship opportunity for Ethan*

The New York Times best-selling author Gretchen Rubin wrote in her book *Better Than Before* that she experienced joy and relief after decluttering her apartment and giving away those material processions that no longer served her.[64] On the show *Tidying up With Marie Kondo*, the Japanese organizing consultant illustrates her methods of organization.[65] Take a look, it might inspire you to take action.

Multitasking

Most experts are against the notion of trying to do more than one thing at a time, citing research findings that multitasking is counterproductive.[66] Our brains can't switch back and forth between different tasks efficiently like a machine. Researchers at the University of Pennsylvania Wharton Business School conducted a study on "the malleability of multitasking perceptions as well as how these perceptions impact performance." They found that "[a]lthough previous literature found that engaging in multiple tasks may diminish performance, … holding the activity constant, the mere perception of multitasking actually increases engagement with the task and improves performance."[67]

Multitasking can work if the different tasks are synergistic (helpful) to each other or involve different parts of your brain. Take the example of walking: you can listen to music, an audiobook, or a podcast. Neither activity affects the other. In fact, you'll walk farther without realizing it because of the auditory entertainment.

The same thing applies to listen to something while doing housework or driving. In the past few years, I have finished twenty audiobooks while driving and walking. The idea of this book came after listening to Gretchen Rubin's *The Happiness Project*.[68] I thought I should write a book for working moms who had been in the trenches so long they had forgotten who they were meant to be.

Other examples of multitasking include doing a few similar tasks at the same time. When your attention wanes, switch to another task. When you become bored again, switch back. This is one of the productivity hacks I tried when studying for three different life science classes while working full time. I'll tell you more about that at the end of this chapter.

Optimize How You Spend Your Time

There are three ways to optimize your time: through saving time, minimizing distractions, and breaking tasks into ministeps and getting them done during your wait time.

1. **Save Time**
   a. Lumping similar activities together saves not only time but also gas. For example, earlier I mentioned

grouping grocery shopping with mailing cards on one trip. With gas prices at $4.50 per gallon (at the time I'm writing), every extra mile driven is money we could have saved.

b. Summarize your findings or conclusion in words right after the completion of the day's task. Write them down in a notebook and date the entry. Don't type on your phone or laptop. Writing triggers brain signals that promote memorization.[69] When working on a large project, make sure you take notes daily, recording the items completed and items still to be done. This makes it easier to keep track of the details within the project, saving you the frustration of digging through old files to find out where you left off.

2. **Minimize Distractions**

a. Schedule a time slot for checking emails and web browsing. Turn your device off once outside of the allowed time. You might experience withdrawal symptoms, such as excessive worries that something terrible might happen while you are "offline." Don't panic; no one has died over this.

b. Set a timer for intense work, then relax once the time is up. Don't worry if the task isn't complete. You can always go back to it when your mind is fresh. This way, you're always at the top of your productivity.

3. **Break Down a Task**

Break a large task into ministeps and get them done during your wait time. I usually schedule Ethan's appointments on the same day as mine so I can get everything done on one trip to the medical office. While we wait, I'll answer emails and Ethan will do his homework. Don't underestimate fifteen or twenty minutes here and there: you can get a lot of things done within that time frame.

When Ethan was in middle school, the campus opened late on Tuesdays at 9:30 a.m. Since he usually arrives around 7:50 a.m., I checked out books he liked from the library and asked him to read while he waited for the school to open. For the three years he studied there, he finished about ten books just by optimizing that wait time.

Planning

Proper planning is essential for productivity. It keeps us on track and minimizes waste of time and resources. With so many distractions around us, we need to know where we are heading at all times. Having a well-thought-out plan gives you a sense of purpose and control. It also allows you to assess your progress and make room for improvement.

I'm a list person. I make a to-do list at the end of each day. As a pharmacist, working in the intensive care unit is stressful. The patients' conditions could change at any minute, and I need to constantly adjust my tasks to meet the care team's needs. It's crucial for me to reflect on the day's events and jot down the items to follow up on later. Without the list, I'll struggle, trying to recall what exactly happened the day before. If I miss anything, it could impact patient care. List-making is the core of my professional life.

I do the same at home. Whenever I receive an invitation or make an appointment, I record it right away on my calendar. This way, I always know how my week or month looks and can easily rearrange if something comes up.

One Day at a Time

Many moms face the challenge of balancing career and motherhood. Many of my friends are tempted to quit their jobs to be full-time moms. I encourage them to stay on the job, even if they have to cut back the hours or switch to another position to accommodate their child-rearing responsibilities.

The world is changing so fast, and we have to keep on learning. Otherwise, we'll feel outdated and irrelevant. Although children are our future, and we must take care of them the best we can, staying in the workforce is essential for our professional growth. It's tremendously difficult to go back to work five years after you leave the job. Your mindset changes; you aren't keeping up with the industry trends, which can make you feel inadequate and out of place. Stay on your job if you can. It not only helps to balance the mind-numbing routine of mothering young children, but also provides you the connection with the outside world. You'll have more to share with your children, and you'll light up their growing minds with infinite knowledge. Never give up learning, even when knowledge seems unnecessary.

For those whose jobs aren't flexible or family friendly, a career change might be in order. It's a daunting task to learn new skills while taking care of your family.

When I decided to become a pharmacist in 2001, I faced significant obstacles. UCSF had been the number one pharmacy school in the country for decades. It was close to home, but the competition was fierce. Other schools were not as competitive but were far away from where I lived. My husband wanted to stay close to his family, so UCSF became my only option. Most of the applicants had majored biochemistry or molecular biology in undergrad, as pharmacy is a chemistry- and biology-focused field. I had only one semester of chemistry and biology in high school. The program prerequisites included general chemistry, organic chemistry, biology, microbiology, and physiology. I was still working full time then. It would take me years to complete the prerequisite if I only took evening classes. Could I do well in these lab sciences after majoring in business and engineering? What if I didn't get accepted after spending all the time and effort needed to learn? I debated back and forth, calculating my odds of success. My desire to be a pharmacist was so strong that I proceeded with my plan.

I enrolled at a local community college and took general chemistry, physiology, and microbiology classes in the evening. A year later, I talked to my boss about working in the evening so I could attend the summer intensive organic chemistry class. The course typically took a whole semester to complete; the intensive class had only six weeks of instruction. On most days, I spent three hours in the lecture followed by three hours of lab, then went to work in the evening.

Soon I received an invitation for an interview at UCSF. One question they asked me was to describe a challenge I faced and how I overcame the difficulties. I talked about my experience at the community college while working full time. I explained how, to make the process less daunting, I divided the big goal into monthly, weekly, and daily goals. Instead of worrying about climbing a steep mountain, I focused on making a small step each day. Before I knew it, I had reached the top. "I suppose that was how a mouse swallowed an elephant," I said.

Two months later, a small envelope with the UCSF logo arrived in my mailbox. I remember feeling the thin paper inside the envelope with my fingers and concluded it must be a rejection letter. I put the envelope away without opening it. My husband had been so supportive and hopeful about my career change that I didn't want to tell him the bad news. When he opened the envelope two days later and rushed downstairs to the laundry room to find me, he hugged me and said, "You got in! I'm so proud of you!"

Nothing is as difficult as it seems. All we have to do is to finish each day's task. Mark it off your calendar and never break that chain.

21

It Takes a Village

NO ONE CAN go at it alone. You'll need people's support.

The support may come in many forms—timely advice when you get stuck, words of encouragement to relieve you from self-doubt, and the loving care that motivates you to push further.

Build your personal support network by offering people what you have first. Let your kindness propagate the chain of events that will improve both of your lives. Don't lend a hand and immediately expect a return. You want to build a relationship, not finish a transaction. Sometimes, people take advantage of your good nature; let them. We don't become poor by giving; we grow greedy by taking.

When you draw up an actionable plan for your goal, take a moment to figure out the logistics. How can you fit your idea into daily life and minimize frictions at work and at home? If your work schedule is flexible, you can negotiate to work a couple of days at home each week. This arrangement will allow you to take care of family needs while meeting the demands of your job. You can then use the free time on your days off to execute your plan. If your work hours are fixed, practice the productivity techniques I showed you to get more done at home so you'll have time to work on your game plan.

Don't let your newfound devotion overwhelm you to the point where you neglect your family and work duties. Remember the three overlapping circles I showed you in Chapter 1? Happiness has three components: health, connection, and satisfaction. Besides pursuing a worthy goal, you also need to maintain loving relationships and optimal emotional and physical health. Take care of your body by living a healthy and active lifestyle. Take care of your mind by focusing on the important things, and let the rest go. Unload the burden of guilt, shame, and jealousy through journaling, and let the words heal you from the inside out. Learn to forgive yourself and others by looking for the beauty in you and around you.

Before you start your dream plan, have a frank conversation with your partner. His support is vital to your success. *Well,* I hear you say, *my husband is the one who says I'm a quitter.* Yes, he can be your ally if you let him.

First of all, he knows you. Before you recount all the occasions he has misunderstood you, remember that he is the one closest to you. He knows you on a molecular level. He knows how you react to people and what ticks you off. He knows all the little habits you aren't even aware of. Sit down and tell him about your goal and action plan. Let him sigh or shake his head, saying "You're crazy." When he's done, tell him you have to be the best for yourself before you can be the best wife to him. When he recites all your past failures, don't stop him.

Listen to what he has to say and then tell him that is why you need his support to make a change. You're tired of living in survival mode. You want to take charge of your life.

He may scratch his head and say, "What is this all about? Are you mad at me or something?" No, you're not mad at him. You're angry at yourself for having waited this long to take action. He will be skeptical of your sudden desire to change, and that is okay. Promise him he'll see a visible change in you in three months. You'll look good and feel better about yourself; you'll yell less at home, and your sex life will improve. Hey, you'll even let people cut in front of you on the road because you're not uptight and angry anymore. Your transformation is good for mankind. If he doesn't believe you, make a bet with him. Ask for a gift the whole family will enjoy—like a road trip to the Yellowstone National Park, or somewhere else none of you has been to. If you fail, just go back to the old routine, knowing you've wasted money on this book. I promised good results but didn't deliver. What does he have to lose?

Talk to your children. Ask them if they want a dream vacation to Yellowstone, seeing wildlife roaming around in a big backyard of trees. Once they get excited, ask them to help you stay on course so you can win the prize. Make it a game, and on the days you don't feel well, they can give you the extra push you need to get back on track.

Tell your partner you'll start making healthy meal plans and bringing the kids out to exercise, and he's welcome to join. If he refuses, leave him be. When you and the children have a great time working out together, he will feel lonely at home, staring at the TV set. After a few weeks, he will tag along without you asking. Researchers at the University of Aberdeen investigated whether having an exercise companion increases the amount of exercise we do. They found the emotional support from a new sports companion was the most effective way to increase the amount of exercise.[70] Encourage your partner to check his lab work and see how fast his health improves through these lifestyle changes.

After you convince your partner that you're onto something good, make a list of the household chores and ask if he could take over some of them to free you up to work on your dream plan. Remember to automate, delegate, eliminate, and prioritize. After gaining his support, show your friends and other family members what you have achieved, and encourage them to implement similar healthy changes. Share your dream plan with them. Having a support network will make you feel less guilty about doing something that seems self-centered. The more people you talk to, the more accountability partners you'll get and the more committed you'll become.

When I first started writing, my husband thought I was crazy.

"You want to be a writer? Why bother? No one reads books anymore."

"That's okay. I'll write for myself," I replied.

Every time he saw me pounding away at the keyboard, he joked about it. "How is it going, my best-selling author?"

Since my son Ethan enjoyed reading, I showed him my chapters and asked for feedback. When my husband walked by and saw us discussing my writing, he would shake his head. Critiquing my work helped Ethan with his own writing. His English teacher often praised his essays. A few months after starting our homegrown literary club, my husband told me he was proud that Ethan had helped his friends edit their writing assignments. I asked my husband if he would be interested in reading my work. He said he would give his honest opinion if I summarized the story for him. (My husband doesn't read novels, but he has a good eye for spotting plot holes and inconsistencies.) When he saw my progress on the book, he offered to take over some household chores so I could concentrate on writing.

You see, even your loved ones won't be able to support your newfound passion right away. It's your job to show them how serious you are about this and what it means for you to reach your goal. If you put in the work every day, soon your effort will drown out the disbelief. They'll come to admire your courage and discipline and will want to help you achieve your dream.

22

A Most Splendid Ride

THANK-YOU FOR TAKING the journey with me through these chapters. At the start of this book, you were disappointed at how life turned out. You wanted more, but you weren't sure what you wanted and how to go about getting it. In "The Mind," you realized you don't have to be perfect to be happy. You can aim for being good enough. You found ways to uncover your strengths and to improve the fit between your strengths and your life. You learned the tools to unload your emotional burden and live true to your values. You saw how a simple way of living could make you happier. You explored the methods of raising flourishing children and the importance of nurturing the love for your partner.

In "The Body," you began your physical transformation. You learned to appreciate your body and make the best of what you have. You followed the four commandments of beauty to enhance your features. No longer shying away from colors, you adopted flattering ways to dress for your body type. You discovered techniques to improve your sleep and workouts to improve your health. You looked beyond the dietary hypes and trends and learned to treat food as medicine. You recognized the benefits of a satisfying sex life and explored the power of physical love.

In "The Path," you examined your old dream and why it was important to you. You drew your growth roadmap by reverse engineering the experts' success. You learned how to maximize your productivity and build a support network to motivate you.

Now, you're ready to embark on the journey to a new life.

Good luck, my friends, I wish you all the very best. No one can predict the future, but I can guarantee you'll meet challenges and setbacks along the way. I want to see you off with these words:

Be prepared to be disappointed, brokenhearted even, when everything seems to go against you. Build a defense system for times like that. Have a mentor guide you through troubles; have your partner or a close friend comfort you; have your accomplishment journal handy to appreciate how much you have already achieved.

Be prepared when things are going too well, when your business is taking off and your talent is in high demand. Don't neglect the other two vital components of happiness—your health and your relationships. Keep everything in balance and share the fruit of your labor with all who have helped you.

Be prepared by having a Plan B. When the situation challenges you to gamble, take a moment to draw up a backup plan. If there's no alternative, don't do it. You don't want to end up with your back against the wall.

Be open to new opportunities. Don't worry if you're good enough. You only become good by doing. Failure is the prequel to growth. Change your struggles into knowledge and turn your mistakes into wisdom.

Be flexible in your approach. When something doesn't work after multiple tries, test a different angle. Read a book, watch video tutorials, talk to people, and learn to draw inspiration from random events. The clues are everywhere; you just have to look for them.

Be optimistic. Your attitude plays a role in your likelihood of success. Happiness is a mindset built on open-mindedness and gratitude. Choosing to see the bright side may just bring you the lucky break you deserve.

Be humble. There is always something you can learn from the person next to you. Pay attention to those with specialized skills. Don't copy their ideas; study their methods instead. Change their approaches to fit your practice and come up with your own creation.

Be you. Stop comparing yourself to other people. Remember, your height doesn't change when you stand next to a giant or a dwarf. You don't have to be perfect—just be the best of you. Think of life as a train ride. We're all heading for the same destination, but everyone sees a different view. Stop looking at life through others' lenses. Find your own horizon. Make your ride the most splendid and memorable.

Acknowledgments

To all the strong women who live on screens,
in books, and in real life.

Your courage, passion, and perseverance are
my inspiration to write.

This book wouldn't exist without the help of the following people.

My deepest gratitude to Dr. Kenneth Atchity for his wisdom and guidance on my literary journey. His academic background and Hollywood film production experience made him the best teacher on what good writing is and how to tell a great story.

My utmost respect for Candace Johnson for her super-logical mind, keen insights, and meticulous work on shaping my words into a book that resonates with you. Her judgment and advice kept my writing sharp and riveting.

My heartfelt thanks to my alpha reader, Hyunmee Corlett. She has read all of my work, from thriller to self-help book, in each revision. Her honesty, kindness, and strong literary sensibility guided me throughout the writing process.

Such a blessing to work with Laura Gianino. Her ambition, ingenuity, and extensive media outreach made it possible for me to share the message of this book with so many of you.

Many thanks to my talented cover designer HikkO for her amazing ability to turn words into art and touch women's hearts.

A special thank-you to Gary Sikorski, Michele Vennard, and Dr. Mohamed Ali for agreeing to my interview requests and sharing their expertise and timely advice for readers of this book. Also, Drs. Sheila Brear and Daphne Miller at the University of California, San Francisco (UCSF) and Dr. Satchin Panda at the University of California, San Diego (UCSD) for sharing their research findings on optimal health.

And my love and gratitude to Chu, for taking over the housework while I slaved away on my laptop, and for taking majestic travel photos and making the tenderest beef brisket. To Ethan, for loving me unconditionally, and never ceasing to amaze me how a growing mind can see through clutter and find beauty in words and life.

About the Author

From an aspiring actress to working for airline executives to becoming a pharmacy professor and a multigenre author, Dr. Ivy Ge has transformed her life while balancing her role as a working mother and a wife.

She writes to inspire women to design their own fate. Her thrillers tell the extraordinary tales of ordinary heroines caught between personal conflicts and national crises. Her self-help books empower women to pursue self-growth outside the role of caregivers. Visit her website https://ivyge.com for more information on how to create the life you love.

Besides traveling, she enjoys practicing hot yoga, horseback riding, and skiing in the mountains in Lake Tahoe, California, with her family.

Questions?

If my message aligns with your organization's vision and culture, reach me at Contact@ivyge.com for speaking engagements, workshops, and bulk order discount.

Enjoy this book? Check out the book's multipurpose companion journal to help you stay focused and efficient.

Can't find answers to your questions in this book? Sign up for free online courses and helpful tips on creating the life you love at https://ivyge.com.

Want to spread the word about this book? Leave a review on Amazon:

1. Scroll to the **Customer Reviews section** on this book page.
2. Click **Write a customer review**.
3. Write your heart out and then click **Submit**.

Finally, stay connected by following my Facebook page at https://www.facebook.com/IvyGeAuthor/, on Twitter at @IvyGeAuthor, and on Pinterest at https://www.pinterest.com/IvyGe/.

Notes

Chapter 2

[1]   Myers-Briggs personality test: https://www.myersbriggs.org, 16 personality factor questionnaire: https://www.16personalities.com/free-personality-test.

[2]   Nicole Kidman's story is on the Stuttering Foundation website: https://www.stutteringhelp.org/content/nicole-kidman.

Chapter 4

[3]   Walker, W. Richard, John J. Skowronski, and Charles P. Thompson. "Life Is Pleasant—and Memory Helps to Keep It That Way!" https://www.apa.org/pubs/journals/releases/gpr-72203.pdf; The original study: http://content.time.com/time/specials/2007/article/0,28804,1631176_1630611_1630586,00.html

Chapter 5

[4]   Pennebacker, James W. "Expressive Writing in Psychological Science." *Sage Journals*, October 29, 2017. https://journals.sagepub.com/doi/10.1177/1745691617707315.

[5]   "Combat Breathing: Use the Same Breathing Techniques as Soldiers." August 23, 2018. *The Spire Health Blog* (blog). https://blog.spire.io/2018/08/23/combat-breathing/.

[6]   Hedges, Kristi. "Stop. Reflect. Try New Things." October 14, 2014. Forbes.com. https://www.forbes.com/sites/work-in-progress/2014/10/14/the-power-of-pause/#2e2cc0087368.

7   Cambridge Dictionary, s.v. "reverse engineer," accessed June 29, 2019. https://dictionary.cambridge.org/us/dictionary/english/reverse-engineering?q=reverse+engineer

8   Lemieux, Cara P. "Brené Brown Talks to The Shriver Report: The Power of Shame on Women Living on the Brink." The Shriver Report (website). http://shriverreport.org/how-to-overcome-shame-when-on-the-brink-brene-brown/.

9   Monroe, Marilyn, and Ben Hecht. 2007. *My Story*. Lanham, Maryland: Taylor Trade Publishing.

Chapter 9

10   I summarized Tony Robbins's talk on the five disciplines of love in "The 5 Disciplines of Love: How to Create Your Ultimate Relationship." TonyRobbins.com (website). Visit his website for full descriptions at https://www.tonyrobbins.com/love-relationships/the-5-disciplines-of-love/

Chapter 10

11   I polled The Knowledge Business Blueprint group on Facebook on June 19, 2019. This is an entrepreneur group created by Dean Graziosi and Tony Robbins in January 2019. The Knowledge Business Blueprint Group, "What is the one thing you wish your parents taught you?" Facebook, June 19, 2019. https://www.facebook.com/groups/knowledgebusiness/.

12   Chua, Amy. *Battle Hymn of the Tiger Mother*. 2011. New York, NY: Penguin.

13   Cambridge Dictionary, s.v. "curiosity," accessed July 16, 2019. https://dictionary.cambridge.org/us/dictionary/english/curiosity

14   Kashdan, Todd B., Ryne A. Sherman, Jessica Yarbro, and David C. Funder. "How are Curious People Viewed and How Do They Behave in Social Situations? From the Perspectives of Self, Friends, Parents, and Unacquainted Observers." https://www.ncbi.nlm.nih.gov/pmc/articles/PMC3430822/.

15   Thompson, Andrea. "Secret of Old Faithful Revealed." June 3, 2008. Live Science (website). For at least the past 135 years, Old Faithful has reliably spewed bursts of steam and hot water every 50 to 90 minutes (the frequency has recently hovered around every 91 minutes), to the wonder of tourists. More than 100,000 eruptions of the geyser have been recorded.

16   Tran, Miribel. "A Stanford Student's Thoughts on Our Recent Suicides." March 13, 2019. Thrive Global (website). https://thriveglobal.com/stories/a-stanford-students-thoughts-on-our-recent-suicides/

Chapter 11

17   "Get the Facts." National Organization for Women (website). https://now.org/now-foundation/love-your-body/love-your-body-whats-it-all-about/get-the-facts/. For further reading, this reference article summarizes the body image trend in the US and listed many related articles: Martin, Jeanne B. "The Development of Ideal Body Image Perceptions in the United States." *Nutrition Today*, Vol 45 No. 3, May/June, 2010. https://pdfs.semanticscholar.org/9baf/87fa4 1962e3454b6365c2900f9202fb896ae.pdf.

18   "Looks Aren't Everything. Believe Me, I'm a Model. Accessed May 22, 2019. https://www.ted.com/talks/cameron_russell_looks_aren_t_everything_believe_me_i_m_a_model?language=en

Chapter 12

19   Jonaitis, Jenna. "These 12 Exercises Will Help You Reap the Health Benefits of Good Posture." September 18, 2019. Healthline.com (website). https://www.healthline.com/health/fitness-exercise/posture-benefits

20   Bleicher, Ariel, Susan Godstone, Dresday Joswig, Anne Kavanagh, et al. "The UCSF Guide to Healthy and Happy Eating." July 2, 2019. University of California San Francisco (website). https://www.ucsf.edu/news/2019/06/414696/ucsf-guide-healthy-and-happy-eating?utm_source=constantcontact&utm_medium=email&utm_campaign=pulsetoday&utm_content=edition101.

21   Military sleep training method is transcribed from Bright Side YouTube video published on October 22, 2018 at https://www.youtube.com/watch?v=g1CWinr5AkI.

Chapter 13

22   Scott, Ellen. "Why Are People So Bothered by Women Putting on Makeup on Public Transport?" January 18, 2017. Metro News (website). https://metro.co.uk/2017/01/18/why-are-people-so-bothered-by-women-putting-on-makeup-on-public-transport-6389234/.

23 Alam, Murad, Anne J. Walter, Amelia Geisler, et al. "Association of Facial Exercise with the Appearance of Aging." Jama Network (website). March 2018. https://jamanetwork.com/journals/jamadermatology/fullarticle/2666801.

24 Gary Sikorski (developer of Happy Face Yoga), in discussion with the author, August 9, 2019.

25 "How to Use Mayonnaise as a Hair Conditioner." June 11, 2019. WikiHow (website). https://www.wikihow.com/Use-Mayonnaise-as-a-Hair-Conditioner.

26 "Did You Know? Interesting Facts about Teeth and Dentistry." Children's Dental Village (website). https://www.childrensdentalvillage.net/patient/resources/interesting-facts/.

27 "Brushing Your Teeth." MouthHealthy.org (website). https://www.mouthhealthy.org/en/az-topics/b/brushing-your-teeth.

28 Berry, Jennifer. "What to Do For Healthy Teeth and Gums." March 14, 2019. Medical News Today (website). https://www.medicalnewstoday.com/articles/324708.php

Cherney, Kristeen. "11 Ways to Keep Your Teeth Healthy." November 13, 2017. Healthline (website). https://www.healthline.com/health/dental-and-oral-health/best-practices-for-healthy-teeth#2.

29 "How CloSYS Works." ClōSys (website). https://closys.com/pages/how-closys-works.

30 Bleicher, Ariel, Susan Godstone, Dresday Joswig, Anne Kavanagh, et al. "The UCSF Guide to Healthy and Happy Eating." July 2, 2019. University of California San Francisco (website). https://www.ucsf.edu/news/2019/06/414696/ucsf-guide-healthy-and-happy-eating?utm_source=constantcontact&utm_medium=email&utm_campaign=pulsetoday&utm_content=edition101.

31 Carey, Clifton M. "Tooth Whitening: What We Now Know." ScienceDirect.com (website). https://doi.org/10.1016/j.jebdp.2014.02.006

32 Tapia, Jose Luis, Alfredo Aguirre. "Oral Friction Hyperkeratosis Clinical Presentation." February 10, 2016. https://emedicine.medscape.com/article/1076089-clinical.

33 Mohamed Ali, DDS, in discussion with the author, September 13, 2019.

34   Spector, Nicole. "Smiling can trick your brain into happiness—and boost your health." November 28, 2017. NBCNews.com (website). https://www.nbcnews.com/better/health/smiling-can-trick-your-brain-happiness-boost-your-health-ncna822591

"Smile: It Could Make You Happier." *Scientific American Mind*, September/October 2009. https://www.scientificamerican.com/index.cfm/_api/render/file/?method=inline&fileID=0B105 1AE-5333-45AB-8D48B58C2F015511.

Chapter 14

35   Abbas, Talia. "11 Expert Tips for Finding the Right Bra Size and Fit." July 23, 2018. Summarized from the article at Self.com (website). https://www.self.com/story/tips-for-finding-the-right-bra-size-and-fit.

36   Dijkstra, Peter D., and Paul T. Y Preenen. "The Red Advantage: The Impact of Red on Combat Sports." 2008. Durham University (website). http://community.dur.ac.uk/red.advantage/index.html/wordpress/research/

37   Cherry, Kendra. "Color Psychology: Does It Affect How You Feel? How Colors Impact Moods, Feelings, and Behaviors." Very Well Mind (website). July 25, 2019. https://www.verywellmind.com/color-psychology-2795824

"The Psychology and Meaning of Colors." ColorPsychology.org (website). https://www.colorpsychology.org/

Kolenda, Nick. "Color Psychology." Nick Kolenda *Psychology and Marketing* (blog). https://www.nickkolenda.com/color-psychology/.

"Psychological Properties of Colours." Colour Affects (website). http://www.colour-affects.co.uk/psychological-properties-of-colours.

38   Haughney, Kathleen for Florida State University. "An Eye for Fashion: Researcher Finds Optical Illusion Garments Can Improve Body Image." November 30, 2016. Science Daily (website). https://www.sciencedaily.com/releases/2016/11/161130141055.htm; https://news.fsu.edu/news/education-society/2016/11/30/eye-fashion-researcher-finds-optical-illusion-garments-can-improve-body-image/.

Ridgway, J. L., J. Parsons, M. Sohn. "Creating a More Ideal Self Through the Use of Clothing: An Exploratory Study of Women's

Perceptions of Optical Illusion Garments." *Clothing and Textiles Research Journal*, 2016; DOI: 10.1177/0887302X16678335.

39 Raes, Bridgette. "Slim Your Body with these Fashion Optical Illusions." November 3, 2011. *Bridgette Raes Style Expert* (blog). https://bridgetteraes.com/2011/11/03/slim-your-body-with-these-fashion-optical-illusions/.

Chapter 15

40 Tara Parker-Pope. "When Sex Leaves the Marriage." New York Times (website). June 3, 2009. https://well.blogs.nytimes.com/2009/06/03/when-sex-leaves-the-marriage/

41 Davis, Michele Weiner. 2003. *The Sex-Starved Marriage: Boost Your Marriage Libido*. New York, New York: Simon & Schuster.

42 Charnetski CJ, Brennan FX. "Sexual frequency and salivary immunoglobulin A (IgA)." *Psychological Reports*. Published June 1, 2004. DOI: 10.2466/pr0.94.3.839-844.

43 Leigh Campbell. "How Your Pelvic Floor Muscles Affect Sex (And Other Things)." HuffPost (website). August 8, 2016. https://www.huffingtonpost.com.au/2016/08/07/how-your-pelvic-floor-muscles-affect-sex-and-other-things_a_21446735/.

44 Nicole Galan. "Does sex provide health benefits?" Medical News Today (website). August 23, 2019. https://www.medicalnewstoday.com/articles/316954.php.

45 Maunder L, Schoemaker D, Pruessner JC. "Frequency of Penile-Vaginal Intercourse is Associated with Verbal Recognition Performance in Adult Women." *Archives of Sexual Behavior*. 2017 Feb;46(2):441-453. DOI: 10.1007/s10508-016-0890-4.

46 Lastella, Michele et al. "Sex and Sleep: Perceptions of Sex as a Sleep Promoting Behavior in the General Adult Population." *Frontiers in Public Health* vol. 7:33. Published Mar 4, 2019. DOI:10.3389/fpubh.2019.00033.

47 Merissa Nathan Gerson. "How Orgasm Could Dull Pain." The Atlantic (website). May 12, 2014. https://www.theatlantic.com/health/archive/2014/05/how-orgasm-could-dull-pain/361470/.

48 Hambach, Anke et al. "The impact of sexual activity on idiopathic headaches: An observational study." *Cephalalgia*, *33*(6), 384–389. Published February 19, 2013. https://doi.org/10.1177/0333102413476374.

49 Rider, Jennifer, Kathryn M. Wilson, Jennifer A. Sinnott, et al. "Ejaculation Frequency and Risk of Prostate Cancer: Updated Results with an Additional Decade of Follow-up." *European Urology*. December 2016, Volume 70, Issue 6, Pages 974–982. https://doi.org/10.1016/j.eururo.2016.03.027.

50 Stanovick, Katie. "Two Dermatologists Tell Us Why Sex Is Actually Good for Your Skin." Business Insider, StyleCaster (website). Feb 22, 2018. https://www.businessinsider.com/dermatologists-explain-why-sex-is-actually-good-for-your-skin-2018-2.

Chapter 16

51 Ingraham, Christopher. "The Absurdity of Women's Clothing Sizes, in One Chart." August 11, 2015. The Washington Post (website). https://www.washingtonpost.com/news/wonk/wp/2015/08/11/the-absurdity-of-womens-clothing-sizes-in-one-chart/.

52 Bleicher, Ariel, Susan Godstone, Dresday Joswig, Anne Kavanagh, et al. "The UCSF Guide to Healthy and Happy Eating." July 2, 2019. University of California San Francisco (website). https://www.ucsf.edu/news/2019/06/414696/ucsf-guide-healthy-and-happy-eating?utm_source=constantcontact&utm_medium=email&utm_campaign=pulsetoday&utm_content=edition101.

Chapter 17

53 Snape, Joel. "Ectomorph, Endomorph and Mesomorph: How To Train for Your Body Type." Coach (website). Sept 1, 2017. September 27, 2017. https://www.coachmag.co.uk/lifestyle/4511/ectomorph-endomorph-or-mesomorph-what-is-your-body-type.

54 Summers, James K., Deborah N. Vivian. "Ecotherapy—A Forgotten Ecosystem Service: A Review." *Front Psychol.* 2018; 9:1389. https://www.ncbi.nlm.nih.gov/pmc/articles/PMC6085576/.

55 Lally, Phillippa, Cornelia H. M., Van Jaarsveld, et al. "How are habits formed: Modelling habit formation in the real world." *European Journal of Social Psychology,* 40, 998–1009 (2010). Published online 16 July 2009 in Wiley Online Library (wileyonlinelibrary.com) DOI: 10.1002/ejsp.674 https://centrespringmd.com/docs/How%20Habits%20are%20Formed.pdf.

56 "Don't Break the Chain—Jerry Seinfeld's Method for Creative Success." The Writers Store (website). https://www.writersstore.com/dont-break-the-chain-jerry-seinfeld/.

57 Izumi Tabata et al. "Effects of moderate-intensity endurance and high-intensity intermittent training on anaerobic capacity and VO2 max." *Medicine & Science in Sports & Exercise* 28(10), 1327-1330. https://journals.lww.com/acsm-msse/Fulltext/1996/10000/Effects_of_moderate_intensity_endurance_and.18.aspx.

58 Tucker, Alexa. "A Sweaty, 24-Minute Cardio HIIT Workout You Can Do in Your Livingroom." September 2, 2016. Self.com (website). https://www.self.com/story/a-sweaty-24-minute-cardio-workout-you-can-do-in-your-living-room.

59 "7 Out of 10 Women Suffer Joint Pain from the Age of 35." Osteoarthritis Foundation International (website). https://oafifoundation.com/en/7-out-of-10-women-suffer-joint-pain-from-the-age-of-35/

60 "The Best Yoga Apps of 2019." Healthline (website). https://www.healthline.com/health/fitness-exercise/top-yoga-iphone-android-apps#daily-yoga

61 Mozes, Alan. "'Hot' Yoga Is No Better for Your Heart: Study." WebMD (website). January 19, 2018. https://www.webmd.com/balance/news/20180119/hot-yoga-is-no-better-for-your-heart-study

62 Video recording of Michele Vennard's 2018 yoga competition at https://www.youtube.com/watch?v=Udrn02WBAUw

63 Michele Vennard in discussion with the author, September 2, 2019.

Chapter 20

64 Rubin, Gretchen. *Better Than Before: What I Learned About Making and Breaking Habits—to Sleep More, Quit Sugar, Procrastinate Less, and Generally Build a Happier Life. 2015.* New York, NY: Broadway Books.

65 *Tidying Up with Marie Kondo.* 2019. Aired February 9, 2019 accessed at https://www.netflix.com/title/80209379.

66 American Psychological Association (website). March 20, 2006. "Multitasking: Switching costs." https://www.apa.org/research/action/multitask.

67 Wharton School of the University of Pennsylvania (website). December 26, 2017. "The Real (and Imaginary) Benefits of Multitasking." https://knowledge.wharton.upenn.edu/article/real-imaginary-benefits-multitasking/.

68 Rubin, Gretchen. "Third Anniversary! Our Most Popular Try-This-at-Home Tips, Happiness Hacks & Favorite Moments," episode 157. *Happier with Gretchen Rubin.* February 22, 2018. https://gretchenrubin.com/podcast-episode/157-happier-third-anniversary.

69 Blatchford, Emily. "Writing by Hand Improves Your Memory, Experts Say." HuffPost. April 21, 2016. https://www.huffingtonpost.com.au/2016/04/21/writing-by-hand-benefits_n_9735384.html.

Chapter 21

70 University of Aberdeen. "A new exercise partner is the key to exercising more." *Science Daily.* October 4, 2016. https://www.sciencedaily.com/releases/2016/10/161004081548.htm.

Made in the USA
Middletown, DE
12 July 2025

10518496R00113